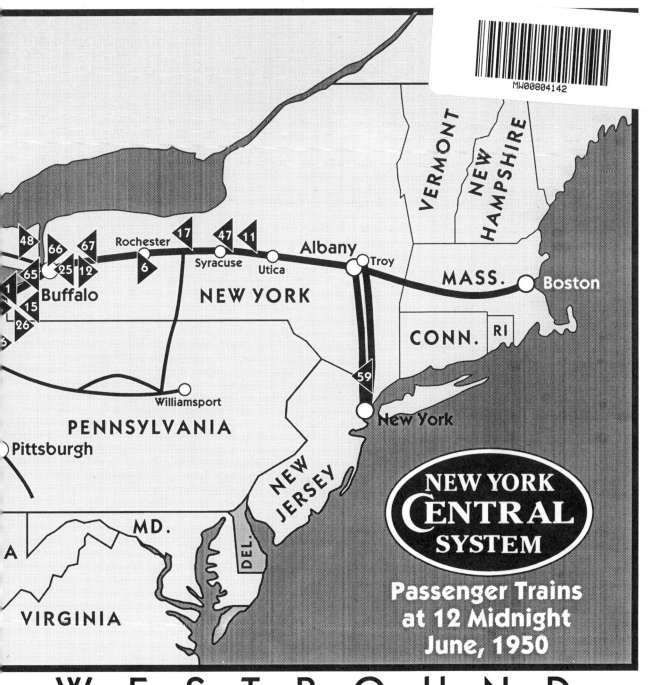

NEW YORK CENTRAL SYSTEM

Passenger Trains at 12 Midnight June, 1950

W E S T B O U N D

The Pacemaker
Westfield, New York

The Advance Commodore Vanderbilt
Dunkirk, New York

The Southwestern Limited
Between Rome and Syracuse, New York

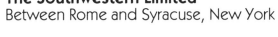

The Detroiter
East Syracuse, New York

The Ohio State Limited
West of Buffalo

The New England States
20 Minutes West of Buffalo, New York

The Commodore Vanderbilt
30 Minutes West of Buffalo, New York

The 20th Century Limited
Buffalo, New York

The Wolverine
Between Syracuse and Rochester, N.Y.

The Chicagoan
10 minutes West of Harmon, New York

New York Central's
Great Steel Fleet
1948-1967

by

Geoffrey H. Doughty

1995
TLC Publishing, Inc.
Route 4, Box 154
Lynchburg, Virginia 24503-9711

Front Cover Illustration: The railroad never sleeps. On any given night in the early 1950s, trains of the Great Steel Fleet converged on Buffalo Central Terminal—midway point of New York Central's cross-system routes—for change of crews, servicing, and exchanging passengers. In this painting by noted railroad artist Andrew Harmantas, a second section of the Chicago-bound *20th Century Limited,* outfitted with one of the prewar *Island*-series observation cars, is being serviced at left. The *New England States,* its E7s pointed eastward toward its Boston destination, is on the adjacent track, and the *Ohio State Limited* pauses several tracks away, en route to Cincinnati. On this night the realities of railroad operations are reflected in the fact that one of the three high-windowed observation cars of the *Southwestern Limited* is substituting for either of the *Plum Brook* or *Fall Brook* cars regularly assigned to the *Ohio State.* Soon all three trains will depart, making room for the parade of other approaching streamliners of the Great Steel Fleet.

© Copyright 1995
TLC Publishing, Inc.

Library of Congress Catalog Number 95-61342
ISBN 1-883089-18-2

Layout and Design by
Kenneth L. Miller, Miller Design & Photography, Salem, Virginia

Printed in USA

Contents

Dedication

To my parents, with love and thanks for the trips aboard The Great Steel Fleet.

Endsheets

Front: System Map by Kenneth L. Miller

Rear: Photo by Bob Yanosey, Collection H. H. Harwood, Jr.

All other material not otherwise credited is the authors collection.

NOW—*World's Largest Fleet* OF NEWLY EQUIPPED TRAINS

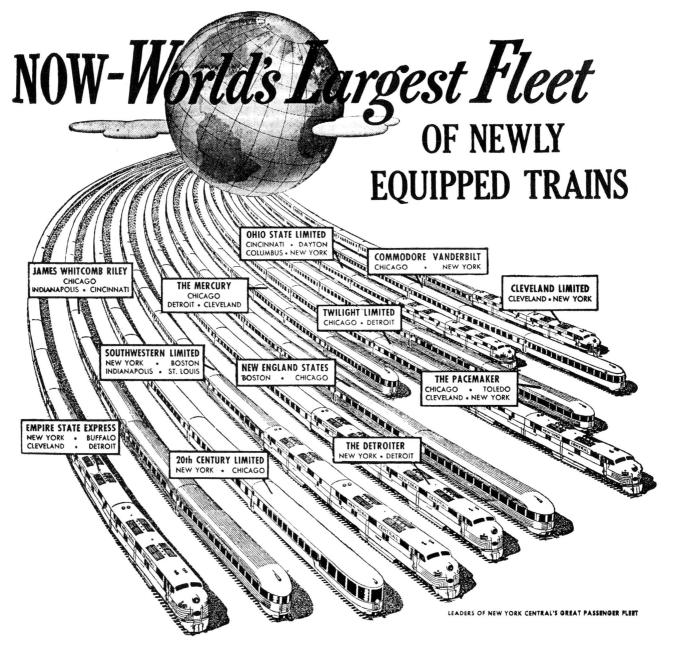

OHIO STATE LIMITED
CINCINNATI • DAYTON
COLUMBUS • NEW YORK

COMMODORE VANDERBILT
CHICAGO • NEW YORK

JAMES WHITCOMB RILEY
CHICAGO
INDIANAPOLIS • CINCINNATI

CLEVELAND LIMITED
CLEVELAND • NEW YORK

THE MERCURY
CHICAGO
DETROIT • CLEVELAND

TWILIGHT LIMITED
CHICAGO • DETROIT

SOUTHWESTERN LIMITED
NEW YORK • BOSTON
INDIANAPOLIS • ST. LOUIS

NEW ENGLAND STATES
BOSTON • CHICAGO

THE PACEMAKER
CHICAGO • TOLEDO
CLEVELAND • NEW YORK

EMPIRE STATE EXPRESS
NEW YORK • BUFFALO
CLEVELAND • DETROIT

THE DETROITER
NEW YORK • DETROIT

20th CENTURY LIMITED
NEW YORK • CHICAGO

LEADERS OF NEW YORK CENTRAL'S GREAT PASSENGER FLEET

...bringing you the NEW in New York Central!

YOU'LL FIND A WORLD OF NEW COMFORT not only on the fleet shown here, but on dozens of other daily trains. Production's caught up with the world's largest orders for reclining-seat coaches, private-room sleeping cars, diners and lounges, plus smooth, new Diesel-electric locomotives. And, all over New York Central, that means new luxury for you!

A WORLD OF DEPENDABILITY AS WELL! You won't find this fleet cancelling trips or landing you at unexpected destinations. Here's travel you can *plan* on with safety and certainty . . in fall weather and *all* weather! For New York Central's dependable Dieseliners get you there, storm or fair . . . and in spacious, air-conditioned comfort all the way.

INFORMATION: CHERRY 8200

WHEREVER YOU GO IN THESE "CENTRAL" STATES *ask your ticket agent to route you via New York Central . . . aboard the world's largest fleet of newly-equipped trains.*

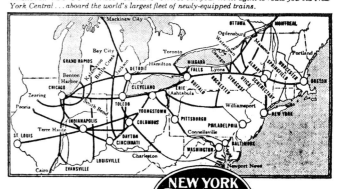

NEW NEW YORK CENTRAL
The Water Level Route—You Can Sleep

NEW YORK CENTRAL SYSTEM

ii

PREFACE

It may become obvious to the reader that this book was truly a labor of love and was not written without a sense of regret. Our society owes a great debt of gratitude to the railroads for they played a vital role in the development of the country and are a source of its wealth. A nation's strength is often measured by its transportation resources-especially its passenger trains.

Many people grow up waving at trains. They don't wave at bus drivers or at airplane pilots, but they wave at locomotive engineers. No other industry has such a following. Passenger trains took on lives of their own; they could be relied upon; people set their watches by their passing.

Up to the early 1950s, the passenger train was a crucial thread in the fabric of the United States. The train connected the cities and towns. Its demise helped erode these bonds and we lost a sense of cohesion.

There were two conflicting points of view about the demise of the passenger train in the 1950s and 1960s. The first postulated that the railroads abandoned the passenger while the second argument claimed that the passenger abandoned (deserted) the train. The truth lies somewhere in between. It was a vicious cycle—one (either one) led to the other— and once started, it became difficult to reverse. Only during the August 1966 airline strike did rail travel experience a sudden and brief rebound, but when the strike was over, the downward spiral resumed.

If any railroad could have made passenger service profitable, certainly New York Central could have. The railroad spent millions of dollars on stations, equipment, property, labor, and advertising. It was a tremendous investment to make the passenger service earn a profit, in spite of all the barriers, and it kept on trying as the losses increased. All too soon, the railroad was in trouble and its great passenger train fleet was sapping its strength. Something had to be done. It had to cut its losses.

To many, in an historic sense (it was, after all, William K. Vanderbilt is credited as saying, "The public be damned!"), the railroad may have been big and impersonal, but the advertising department and employees made the patron feel like an honored guest who was always welcome. That attention and good will created a bond that was weakened only by the convenience of the car and airplane.

I wrote this book to savor both the intangibles of travel and the hardware which are the genesis of great memories. It is not intended to be a comprehensive account of New York Central's long distance passenger operations, which were on an enormous scale, but rather a representative overview of them. I chose to cover the passenger trains which New York Central itself promoted in its advertising as the "world's largest passenger fleet." It is only one chapter in the history of New York Central operations, but a remarkable one.

The Great Steel Fleet of 1948-1967 will bring back memories for some and for others it will offer a glimpse at how first-class travel was defined and experienced. Either way, I hope you enjoy the ride.

Geoffrey H. Doughty

NYCSHS Collection

The Great Steel Fleet. La Salle Street Station, July 10, 1949. From left: *The Wolverine, The Pacemaker, The New England States, The Commodore Vanderbilt* and the *20th Century Limited.*

ACKNOWLEDGEMENTS

There are many people who have contributed their time, expertise, as well as photographs from their collections for which mere acknowledgement is small repayment for their generosity. Some stepped forward to help even though we had never met.

Both Jack Swanberg and Theodore Shrady, graduates of NYC's management training program, gave unselfishly of their time to help me locate photographs, not only from their collections, but in others as well. Despite their busy schedules, they found time to work on my behalf. Their advice and collaboration was most useful and made this project enjoyable.

In a similar fashion, Dr. Louis A. Marre enthusiastically produced numerous photographs relevant to the subject matter without hesitation in spite of the demands of his schedule and responsibilities. He has proven to be an astute historian as well as a distinguished professor of English.

David Randall of RPC graciously consented for us to include information derived from his compilation of ACF, Budd and Pullman-Standard cars.

Victor Baird willingly offered photographs and sought out photographs in other collections, including those of Arthur Shull, Jr. who also did not hesitate to lend photographs. These individuals are credits to the network of rail photographers whose work complements this project.

The same can be said of Wallace Abbey, Herb Harwood, Jay Williams, and Jeffrey Smith who took the time to locate and lend photographs. Richard Stoving dug through the New York Central System Historical Society's cataloged negatives and printed pertinent copies for inclusion in this volume in spite of demanding schedule.

Charles Smith, president of the NYCSHS advised on certain technical matters and secured permission for inclusion of relevant data. His technical expertise was extremely valuable and he was most generous with his time.

Albert Hassett, Jr., Hugh T. Guillaume, and John Horvath graciously consented to have their articles reprinted from the NYCSHS newsletter, *Central Headlight*, which greatly enhanced the information contained in this book. Robert Wayner was also very generous of his time and suggestions regarding technical information.

Several persons, such as the late Richard Cook, Sr., sent me photographs for inclusion and offered encouragement for its completion. Ed Galvin and Thom Colkitt encouraged and inspired my undertaking this project and offered helpful advice during the course of its writing. My mentor and dear friend, Sidney Clark, proofed the manuscript and offered ways to improve it. Richard Sprague, another respected and valued friend, made helpful suggestions and helped focus my thoughts.

My publisher, Tom Dixon, even when suggesting yet *another* project for the book, was most patient and understanding. His advice and support were crucial, not to mention his enthusiasm which seemed to know no bounds.

The assistance of Ken Miller was crucial as I had to rely on his knowledge of the subject as well as his good judgement and expertise. His patience was most appreciated.

Clyde and Sue McCulley, along with Richard Hurst, pursued leads and gathered information for me. Jeff Gehm and Matt Walter actually went out on location to shoot photographs! Victor Hand graciously made the time out of his incredibly busy schedule (between countries!) to select some of the finest photos in this volume. Brian West provided, at a moments notice, many previously unpublished photos of NYC equipment in Canada.

How does one adequately thank these people?

There are many people to whom I owe a debt of gratitude for their time and consideration. These individuals consist of my parents, aunts and uncles, and close family friends, all of whom I ingraciously imposed upon when I was a young boy, and who were patient enough to take me down to the station to watch the trains. Many are gone now and I regret that they are not able to witness the fruit of their efforts and generosity.

The late Richard Overton, for example: historian, educator and author, close family friend and "uncle," served as an inspiration throughout the writing of this book. I will be forever grateful to all for their encouragement.

This book would not have been completed without the invaluable assistance, hard work and dedication of Wanda Worrey who spent days as well as nights meticulously putting the manuscript on a 3-1/2" Macintosh computer disk. She enthusiastically attacked each draft and cheerfully corrected mistakes and made further additions, and only once threatened bodily harm to the author.

My wife, Pamela, is deserving of special mention for allowing me to transport myself back into another era. She forgave my mental and physical absences and tolerated my enthusiasm as the book progressed. She was patient, understanding, and never once mentioned divorce—or asked me to take the dogs for a walk while I was working.

Any writer would be fortunate to have people such as these as a support group. I have been blessed by their association and I have greatly have enjoyed working with them. Their contributions are gratefully acknowledged and for each my deep sense of appreciation goes beyond words.

H. H. Harwood Jr.

"To travel hopefully is a better thing than to arrive."
- Robert Louis Stevenson

NEW YORK CENTRAL SYSTEM

From Head Start...

—to Happy Ending—

You get more vacation relaxation on NEW YORK CENTRAL

Weatherproof Start! Why let stormy skies delay your start? Leave on time, in the all-weather safety and comfort of a New York Central Dieseliner.

Cool Off Right Off! No waiting to reach mountains or shore. You're air-cooled all the way in New York Central's coaches, Pullmans, lounges, diners.

See More as You Go! The scenic Hudson and Mohawk rivers, Berkshires and Great Lakes roll by your picture window, as you relax on New York Central.

Many Happy Returns! Why travel a way that gets you home tired? For a happier return, go New York Central...and get back with vacation vim intact!

THE GREAT STEEL FLEET 1948-1967

When one looks at pictures of passenger trains, it is easy to forget that in more than one sense they were a means to an end. For all their elegance and style, the passenger trains of the glory years were aimed at capturing a transportation market, just one of many the railroads sought. They were used to bolster revenues (approximately 15% of New York Central's total revenue in the early 1950s) by luring the public, as well as potential freight customers, to the rails with the quality of service.

The New York Central (NYC) was an immense railroad—a system after 1935—operating on slightly over 10,000 miles of track in ten states and two Canadian provinces, and its passenger trains were a reflection of its overall service and prestige. NYC, therefore, didn't just operate passenger trains, it ran what it called a "Great Steel Fleet." It's not surprising that NYC with an established heritage of exceptional passenger service would invest huge resources and devote time and energy to capture and retain what was then considered an important market.

One must keep the "Great Steel Fleet" in the context of the times. Long distance travel was accomplished mostly by two modes in 1945, on land by rail and on the oceans by gigantic luxury liners which catered to almost any whim of the person who could afford the tariff. Travel took time, and during those hours when a passenger was in the custody of the host carrier it was expected that the patron would be transported in comfort, fed well and delivered to his or her destination safely, rested and on time. Accomplishing this task in a style and manner which would make its patrons feel privileged, if not a part of royalty, became one of the marketing tools of NYC's passenger traffic department.

The "Great Steel Fleet" originated in the early part of the twentieth century with the conversion to all-steel cars, but gained new prominence in the 1930s with the dawning of the streamline era. Even while the term was used in company advertising through the 1930s, oddly enough it was not used much after 1946. Still, the term became generally accepted and associated with the many trains operated by NYC as the railroad's marketing department moved into high gear.

With the Second World War drawing to a close in 1945, NYC turned its attention to the postwar era and the need to rehabilitate its aging and tired fleet of cars. While some were less than ten years old, they had been tested to their limit trying to keep pace with the demands of the wartime economy.

The first postwar cars were ordered in 1944 and a larger second order followed in December 1945. The passenger traffic department began putting together a strategy to capture the passenger trade within their markets and to publicize the new services even before the new cars arrived in order to get one step ahead of their competition, the Pennsylvania Railroad and its pre-war "Fleet of Modernism." Nobody had the slightest clue about the

NYCSHS Collection

The historic rivalry between the Pennsylvania and the New York Central is exemplified by this famous photo of the "Great Race" between the *Broadway Limited* and the *20th Century Limited*.

future of airline travel or the federal interstate highway system at this point. There was no reason not to pick up where they left off in 1941 when NYC had inaugurated the new streamlined, stainless steel *Empire State Express* on the same day Pearl Harbor was attacked.

At first the new trains were called "dreamliners" with advertisements extolling the virtues of the luxurious caravans. But somehow only the term Great Steel Fleet seemed to accurately describe the new service while simultaneously creating a link with its heritage.

NYC had its fiercest competition from its oldest rival, the Pennsylvania Railroad and there the bid for passenger traffic boiled down to a serious corporate horse race, typified by the age old phrase, "anything you can do, I can do better."

A horse race it was, with new diesel power from no less than four manufacturers leading the crack limiteds of the New York Central. The trains offered the latest products from Pullman-Standard, Budd and American Car and Foundry (ACF) with only the best creature comforts. While the new equipment arrived over the course of several years between 1948 to 1953, NYC trains were sent forth on new and often faster schedules to fill the traveling needs of those on business and pleasure.

Some estimates place the cost of the new equipment at over fifty million dollars. This was quite an investment, especially for 1948, which revealed confidence in the passenger train's future.

In all, NYC ordered 239 cars from Budd, 354 from Pullman-Standard, and 128 from ACF. These cars were fielded in more than 130 trains across the system, augmented, of course, by the refurbished cars from the pre-

N.Y.C. to Re-Equip 28 Trains with Streamlined Cars in 1948

The New York Central will completely re-equip 28 of its principal passenger trains this year with streamlined cars, Gustav Metzman president of the road said this week. Almost as many new cars as are intended for use in the new streamliners will be added to numerous other New York Central trains, he added. This progress, Mr. Metzman continued, is made possible by a steady stream of deliveries of new equipment ordered as long ago as 1944.

The following daily trains were named as destined to be equipped this year with new streamlined cars: the "Twentieth Century Limited" the "Commodore Vanderbilt" and the "Pacemaker" between New York and Chicago; the "New England States" between Boston, Massachusetts, and Chicago; the "Ohio State Limited" between New York and Cincinnati, Ohio; the "Cleveland Limited" between New York and Cleveland, Ohio; the "Detroiter" between New York and Detroit, Michigan; the "Wolverine" between New York and Michigan points; the "Genesee" between New York and Buffalo, New York; the "Southwestern Limited" between New York and St. Louis, Missouri; a twilight streamliner between Cleveland and Chicago; a dayliner between Pittsburgh, Pennsylvania, and Buffalo; and the "Twilight Limited" and the "Motor City" between Detroit and Chicago.

(Excerpted from Railway Age)

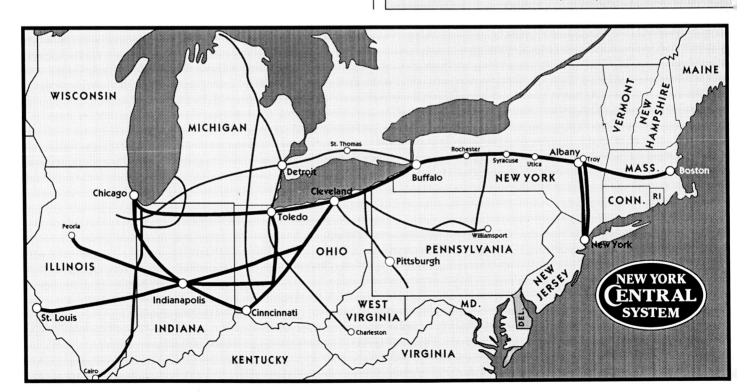

vious Pullman-Standard orders of 1938-40.

To outfit these trains: New York Central ordered, from Budd: 60 coaches; 9 twin-unit diner/kitchen/ lounge cars (18 cars); 12 baggage/crew dormitories; 13 buffet/lounges (variously termed over the next twenty years); 12 dining cars; 18 "grill" dining cars; 13 parlor/observation cars; 40 of the 10-roomette/6-double bedroom sleeping cars (10-6); 11 of the 6-double bedroom/lounge cars; 31 of the 22-roomette cars; and 7, in two different styles, 5-double bedroom/observation/lounge cars for the *New England States* (two); *Ohio State Limited* (two); and *Southwestern Limited* (three).

From Pullman: 153 stainless steel coaches (delivered in 1946); 9 baggage dormitory cars; 4 twin dining car sets - two with kitchen/dormitory for the *20th Century Limited*; 2 with kitchen/lounge for the *Commodore Vanderbilt*; 7 diners; 2 buffet/lounge cars containing a spacious lounge, barbershop, train secretary space and shower, also for the *20th Century Limited*; 45 of the 22-roomette cars; 97 of the 10-roomette/6-double bedroom cars; 16 of the 6-bedroom/lounge cars; 14 of the 12-double bedroom cars; 3 "look out lounge" observation cars (2 for the *20th Century Limited*; 1 stainless steel sheathed car for the joint *New Royal Palm* pool service); and in 1950, 4 more twin-unit diner/kitchen/dormitory cars were bought from Pullman-Standard, part of a canceled order from the Chesapeake and Ohio.

The ACF order was confined to head end equipment; 22 baggage/coach cars; 6 mail baggage and 100 baggage cars. The latter baggage cars survived into the 1990s. During the transition period, it was quite common to see standard ("heavyweight") equipment mixed into the consists of the new trains, but as the new cars arrived, the trains became more consistent in appearance.

In anticipation of the arrival of the new equipment, the 1938-era cars were slowly refurbished in 1946 and 1947 and repainted (first with a reversed gray - dark on top and bottom, light gray with pinstripes in the window band, then a second repainting when the pinstripes were removed). These cars were placed in service and later integrated into the consists of the secondary trains, although for a time the 1938-40 *20th Century Limited* cars would be assigned to the second section of that train, the *Commodore Vanderbilt* and the *Advance Commodore*, as well as the *Southwestern Limited* as demand necessitated. Some were refurbished to be included with the new 1948 *20th Century Limited* train sets.

Older streamlined cars and (as they arrived) the new cars would be assigned or rotated through the transcontinental train service operated jointly with the Santa Fe, Burlington, Chicago & North Western/Union Pacific (later the Milwaukee Road/Union Pacific) and the Rock Island/Southern Pacific.

The transcontinental service began during a time when NYC was the focus of a proxy fight for control by Robert R. Young, Chairman of the Chesapeake and Ohio Railway, who stated in a much-publicized advertisement that a hog could travel coast to coast without changing trains, but people couldn't.

Recognizing the logic of this claim, NYC, beginning in 1946, and for the next 12 years, exchanged sleeping cars between the *Super Chief* and *Chief* and the *20th Century Limited*; the *Los Angeles Limited* and the *Advance Commodore Vanderbilt* (Westbound) and *Lake Shore Limited* (Eastbound) and later the *Wolverine*; the *San Francisco Overland Limited* and the *Chicagoan* (Westbound)/*Lakes Shore* (Eastbound); the *Golden State Limited* and the *Chicagoan* (Westbound)/*Advance Commodore Vanderbilt* (Eastbound); and the *California Zephyr* and the *Lake Shore Limited*.

There was also connecting service through St. Louis between the *Southwestern Limited* and the *Meteor* and *Texas Special* of the Missouri-Kansas-Texas Railroad and with the *Texas Eagle* of the Missouri Pacific. All these services were intended to make travel on the train seem convenient and comfortable if not elegant. On the negative side, the schedules were sometimes confusing.

With the re-equipping of the trains in 1948, the passenger traffic department of NYC set out to schedule the new trains with the operating department so the trains would run on time and with a minimum of conceivable delay when making connecting service. In 1948, NYC ran a mix of Pullman-leased and railroad-owned equipment, all of which NYC maintained. With cars going to the far corners of the system, the task of cycling the cars through a maintenance schedule between runs must have been formidable. It was this practical side of railroading which quickly necessitated the breakup of uniform Budd or Pullman-Standard consists, although the *20th Century Limited* and *Commodore Vanderbilt* were spared.

The "Great Steel Fleet" went through some major realignments in the post-war era. Fleet equipage experienced a metamorphosis between 1947 and 1953 at which point the vast majority of the old standard cars had been replaced, although a few heavyweight diners and sleepers would, on occasion, show up in a consist after that until 1957.

Schedules remained fairly stable after 1948 until 1956 when the effects of competition from the airlines and the highways began to manifest itself. Two years later NYC reacted abruptly to the realities of the public's travel preferences and the most notable change in service occurred: the addition of coaches on the Great Steel Fleet's flagship, the *20th Century Limited*. Other major realignments occurred in 1959, 1966, and finally in 1967 when the last two schedule changes occurred a month apart.

First impressions had a lot to do with NYC's passenger operations. Often a trip on a train began when the passenger stepped into one of the railroad's many grand cathedral-like terminals. Cities such as Boston, New York, Albany, Syracuse, Rochester, Buffalo, Cleveland, Chicago, Cincinnati, Indianapolis, St. Louis, to name but a few, were places where passengers received their first glimpse of first-rate rail passenger travel. What better way could there be to begin a journey than from a *Grand* Central Terminal?

Smaller cities rated these secular temples as well. The Boston and Albany Railroad (an NYC subsidiary), in cooperation with the New Haven Railroad, built stations in Worcester, Springfield and Pittsfield in a similar fashion. When patrons walked through the oak doors they were entering another world—one of opulence, grandeur, and luxury.

Red Caps hustled baggage to and from the trains; taxi cabs delivered and picked up patrons. There were restaurants, soda shops, newsstands—all the services the traveler might need before or after a journey on the Great Steel Fleet. It was, after all, a great adventure.

An appreciation of NYC's Great Steel Fleet operations can be accomplished through a brief review of the system timetables of the trains which carried sleeping cars and which provided lounge and dining services.

The April 1949 system timetable (Form 1001) listed 136 trains in 71 tables, including services to San Antonio, San Francisco, Los Angeles, Miami, and St. Petersburg.

By April 1955, the number of trains listed had dropped slightly to 114 trains in 54 timetables.

In 1957, one year before the restructuring, the Form 1001 listed 115 trains in 48 timetables with the last vestige of transcontinental service to Los Angeles and San

What better way to begin a journey than from a **Grand** Central Terminal. April 22, 1954.

Francisco (discontinued in February 1958).

With the April 1958 schedule change the number of crack limiteds fell to 83 trains listed in 44 tables.

Trimming continued unabated and by April 1963 the timetable listed 46 trains in 18 tables. Four years later in April 1967, there were 24 trains left covered in 6 tables. The November 1967 Form 1001 remained essentially the same, but with the Penn Central merger on the immediate horizon, NYC combined what trains were left in December 1967 and listed 8 trains in 10 tables on a single foldout sheet.

Operating the Great Steel Fleet was a complex undertaking. A person traveling from New York to St. Louis may not have had to change trains, but his sleeper may have been cut out of the train at Cleveland or Buffalo and put into another. The switching operations called for hooking a switch engine on the rear (often the observation car) to exchange cars or having the head end pull away so cars could be set off or cut out, all of which was time consuming and costly. Then the cars had to cycle through movement to other cities so there would be a minimum of "deadheading" (non-revenue moves).

To the average passenger it seemed very simple. One would board the train at Grand Central and the next day step off in St. Louis. Actually, if one were to closely examine the operations across the system it would quickly become apparent that it took the resources of a giant organization to make it all work as smoothly as a Swiss timepiece.

In order to grasp an appreciation of the staffing requirements, consider that a railroad is a highly structured, military-like, class-conscious, and a very labor-intensive business whose primary purpose is to make a profit. Passenger trains historically have not been profitable. A particular train, such as the *20th Century Limited*, may have earned a profit in any particular year, but it was always marginal at best and that profit was predicated on there being a train filled to capacity (or nearly so) whose gross revenues would go beyond mere coverage of expenses.

And there were a lot of expenses. For example, a limited operating between Chicago and New York consisting of 15 cars (coaches, lounge car, twin-unit diner and sleepers), would normally require a train staff of approximately 20 persons: porters—one for each sleeper; coach attendants; lounge attendant; and dining car staff—about a dozen including waiters, cooks and steward. The entire train staff would be there to serve passengers for the entire journey.

The train crew consisted of the operating people who were required to run the train from one part of NYC to the other. In this example, labor contracts and, therefore, operating practices dictated that a train crew operating between Chicago and New York (and vice versa) could run 100 miles (approximately) and their work day would be finished. This was the infamous "basic day" rule. This rule necessitated crew changes every 100-150 miles, which on NYC meant crew changes at Elkhart, Indiana; Toledo and Cleveland, Ohio; Buffalo, Syracuse, Albany and Harmon (engine crews only), New York. Since the average train crew consisted of an engineer, fireman, conductor, assistant conductor, a brakeman and a trainman, that meant that forty-four train crew members were required to get the train "over the road."

This modest example would require 64 persons who just got the train to its destination. Add to that the number of persons in the commissary who provisioned the dining car with food and drink, the car cleaners, the switching crews who assembled the train at its origin or who cut in or cut out cars at intermediate points, car inspec-

H. H. Harwood Jr.

*-1 electric No. 221 backs onto a St. Louis-Cleveland train at Linndale in August, 1952. At ight is a reminder why the P-1 electrics have only a short time left in Cleveland.

QUICK REFERENCE TIME TABLES

NEW YORK—BOSTON—CHICAGO

READ DOWN

	PACE-MAKER R1	COMM. V'BILT R67	20th CENTURY Ex. Sat. ★25	NEW ENG. STATES R27	WOLV-ERINE 17	CHI-CAGOAN 59 Ex. Sat.	IRO-QUOIS 35	CHI-CAGOAN 29 Sat. Only
	PM	PM	PM		PM	PM	PM	PM
Lv NEW YORK (E.T.) Ar	3 30	A 5 30	6 00	......	6 15	9 15	......	11 05
Lv BOSTON (E.T.) Ar	11 45	↓	8 45	3 15	↓	......	7 45	......
Ar CHICAGO (C.T.) Lv (La Salle St. Station)	7 40	8 30	8 45	9 35	11 50	2 50	5 15	4 15
	AM	AM	AM	AM	AM	PM	PM	PM

READ UP

	N.Y. SPL. 44	5th AVE. SPL. 6	WOLV-ERINE R8	NEW ENG. STATES R28	COMM. V'BILT R68	20th CENTURY Ex. Sat. ★26	PACE-MAKER 2	CHI-CAGOAN 90
	AM	AM	AM		AM	AM	PM	PM
Ar NEW YORK (E.T.) Lv	7 10	7 20	8 45	......	9 00	9 30	12 40	7 25
Ar BOSTON (E.T.) Lv	10 00	10 00	10 55	......	......	......	3 50	11 00
Lv CHICAGO (C.T.) Ar	C 10 00	12 01	1 55	2 20	A 4 00	4 45	6 20	11 00
	AM	PM	PM	PM	PM	PM	PM	PM

★—20th Century Limited-De Luxe All Pullman   C—Leaves from Central Station.   R—Coach Seats Reserved.   A—On Saturdays leaves New York 6:00 p.m. and leaves Chicago 4:30 p.m.

NEW YORK—BOSTON—CLEVELAND

READ DOWN

	EMPIRE STATE RP51	OHIO STATE R15	CLEVE. LTD. 57 Ex. Sat.	NORTH STAR 21 Sat. Only	CHI-CAGOAN 59 Ex. Sat.	IRO-QUOIS 35	CHI-CAGOAN 29 Sat. Only
	AM	PM	PM	PM	PM	PM	PM
Lv NEW YORK (E.T.) Ar	9 00	4 00	8 15	8 30	9 15	......	11 05
Lv BOSTON (E.T.) Ar	A 7 00	11 45	5 30	5 30	......	7 45	......
Ar CLEVELAND (E.T.) Lv	8 50	3 26	7 50	10 10	9 05	11 51	10 49
	PM	AM	AM	AM	AM	AM	AM

READ UP

	KNICKER-BOCKER 24	CHI-CAGOAN 90	EMPIRE STATE RP50	5th AVE. SPL. 6	CLEVE. LTD. 58 Ex. Sat.	NEW ENG. STATES R28
	PM	PM	PM	AM	AM	AM
Ar NEW YORK (E.T.) Lv	12 40	7 25	9 30	7 20	7 55	10 55
Ar BOSTON (E.T.) Lv	3 50	6 27	9 40	10 00	9 00	9 33
Lv CLEVELAND (E.T.) Ar	12 25			7 20		
	AM	AM	AM	PM	PM	PM

RP—Coach and Parlor Car Seats Reserved.   R—Coach Seats Reserved.   A—Boston connection operates except Sunday.

NEW YORK—BOSTON—DETROIT

READ DOWN

	EMPIRE STATE RP51	WOLV-ERINE 17	DETROITER R47 Ex. Sat.
	AM	PM	PM
Lv NEW YORK (E.T.) Ar	9 00	6 15	7 25
Lv BOSTON (E.T.) Ar	A 7 00	3 15	7 00
Ar DETROIT (E.T.) Lv	10 25	7 00	8 00
	AM	AM	AM

READ UP

	EMPIRE STATE RP50	N.Y. SPL. 44	DETROITER R48
	PM	AM	AM
Ar NEW YORK (E.T.) Lv	9 30	7 10	8 45
Ar BOSTON (E.T.) Lv	↑	10 00	8 30
Lv DETROIT (E.T.) Ar	8 30	6 00	8 30
	AM	AM	AM

RP—Coach and Parlor Car Seats Reserved.   A—Boston connection operates except Sunday.   R—Coach Seats Reserved.

NEW YORK—MONTREAL

READ DOWN

	LAUREN-TIAN 55	MONT. LTD. 61
	AM	PM
Lv NEW YORK (E.T.) Ar	10 00	11 25
Ar MONTREAL (E.T.) Lv	7 50	9 00
	PM	AM

READ UP

	LAUREN-TIAN 134	MONT. LTD. 62
	AM	AM
Ar NEW YORK (E.T.) Lv	8 45	7 40
Lv MONTREAL (E.T.) Ar	9 55	10 20
	AM	PM

NEW YORK—BOSTON—TORONTO

READ DOWN

	DE WITT CLINTON 95	CLEVE. LTD. 57 Ex. Sat.	NORTH STAR 21 Sat. Only	TUSCA-RORA 99 Ex. Sat.	CHI-CAGOAN 29 Sat. Only
	AM	PM	PM	PM	PM
Lv NEW YORK (E.T.) Ar	7 40	8 15	8 30	11 45	11 05
Lv BOSTON (E.T.) Ar		5 30	5 30	↓	↓
Ar TORONTO (E.T.) Lv	9 00	8 45	8 45	12 30	12 30
	PM	AM	AM	AM	AM

READ UP

	DE WITT CLINTON 96	INT. ST. EXP. 46	CLEVE. LTD. 58 Ex. Sat.	WOLV-ERINE 8 Sat. Only
	PM	AM	AM	AM
Ar NEW YORK (E.T.) Lv	11 30	......	7 55	8 45
Ar BOSTON (E.T.) Lv	↑	10 00	↑	↑
Lv TORONTO (E.T.) Ar	11 30	6 45	8 40	8 40
	AM	AM	AM	AM

BOSTON—BUFFALO

READ DOWN

	EMPIRE RP51 Ex. Sun.	BERK-SHIRE 49	NEW ENG. STATES R27	INT. STATE EXP. 33	IRO-QUOIS 35
	AM	AM	PM	PM	PM
Lv BOSTON (E.T.) Ar	7 00	11 45	3 15	5 30	7 45
Lv SPRINGFIELD (E.T.) Ar	9 03	2 30	5 31	7 50	10 25
Ar BUFFALO (E.T.) Lv	4 55	11 05	1 39	4 07	7 40
	PM	PM	AM	AM	AM

READ UP

	BERK-SHIRE 78	CHI-CAGOAN 90 Ex. Sun.	CHI-CAGOAN 90 Sun. Only	INT. STATE EXP. 46
	PM	PM	PM	AM
Ar BOSTON (E.T.) Lv	3 50	9 00	10 00	10 00
Ar SPRINGFIELD (E.T.) Lv	1 15	6 45	7 20	7 20
Lv BUFFALO (E.T.) Ar	4 49	10 40	10 40	11 30
	AM	AM	AM	PM

RP—Coach and Parlor Car Seats Reserved.   R—Coach Seats Reserved.

NEW YORK—BOSTON—COLUMBUS—DAYTON—CINCINNATI

READ DOWN

	CLEVE. LTD. 57-423 Ex. Sat.	OHIO STATE R15
	PM	PM
Lv NEW YORK (E.T.) Ar	8 15	4 00
Lv BOSTON (E.T.) Ar	5 30	11 45
Ar COLUMBUS (E.T.) Lv	10 32	7 25
Ar DAYTON (E.T.) Lv	12 14	8 40
Ar CINCINNATI (E.T.) Ar	1 30	
	PM	PM

READ UP

	OHIO STATE R16	CHI-CAGOAN 442-90
	AM	PM
Ar NEW YORK (E.T.) Lv	9 20	7 25
Ar BOSTON (E.T.) Lv	12 55	9 00
Lv COLUMBUS (E.T.) Ar	7 47	12 28
Lv DAYTON (E.T.) Ar	6 06	11 00
Lv CINCINNATI (E.T.) Ar	5 00	
	AM	

R—Coach Seats Reserved.

NEW YORK—BOSTON—CLEVELAND—INDIANAPOLIS—ST. LOUIS

READ DOWN

	CLEVE. LTD. 57-11 Ex. Sat.	OHIO STATE R15
	PM	PM
Lv NEW YORK (E.T.) Ar	8 15	4 00
Lv BOSTON (E.T.) Ar	5 30	11 45
Lv CLEVELAND (E.T.) Ar	A 8 30	3 50
Ar INDIANAPOLIS (C.T.) Lv	12 45	8 10
Ar ST. LOUIS (C.T.) Lv	5 40	1 20
	PM	PM

READ UP

	KNICK-BOCKER R24	CLEVE. LTD. 12-58 Ex. Sat.
	PM	AM
Ar NEW YORK (E.T.) Lv	12 40	7 55
Ar BOSTON (E.T.) Lv	3 50	10 55
Ar CLEVELAND (E.T.) Lv	11 57	8 35
Lv INDIANAPOLIS (C.T.) Ar	5 30	2 00
Lv ST. LOUIS (C.T.) Ar	1 00	9 30
	AM	AM

R—Coach Seats Reserved.   A—Operates Daily Cleveland—St. Louis.

 FOR COMPLETE SCHEDULES AND INTERMEDIATE SERVICE SEE CONDENSED AND DETAILED TABLES IMMEDIATELY FOLLOWING.

Please,—Don't be a "NO SHOW"

A "no show" is the person who reserves accommodations and then fails to cancel the reservation when plans are changed.

"No Shows" have two very serious effects on rail transportation—

1. They prohibit other passengers from purchasing the space because the diagram shows the space sold.
2. The railroad loses much needed revenue.

Your kind consideration and cooperation will permit us to serve other patrons and not have the space go unused.

QUICK REFERENCE TIME TABLES

NEW YORK—ALBANY—SYRACUSE—ROCHESTER—BUFFALO

Westbound (EASTERN TIME)	DE WITT CLINTON 96	EMPIRE STATE R51	LAUREN- TIAN 55	HUDSON RIVER SPL. 151	MO- HAWK 39	PACE- MAKER 1	OHIO STATE LTD. R15	HEN- DRICK HUDSON 167	WOLV- ERINE 17	UP- STATE SPL. 119	CLEVE. LTD. 57 Ex. Sat.	NORTH STAR 21 Sat. Only	CHI- CAGOAN 59 Ex. Sat.	IRO- QUOIS 35	CHI- CAGOAN 29 Sat. Only	TUSCA- RORA 99 Ex. Sat.
	AM	AM	AM		PM	PM	PM	PM	PM	PM	PM	PM	PM	PM	PM	PM
Lv NEW YORK	7 40	9 00	10 00	12 15	12 50	3 30	4 00	4 40	6 15	B 6 25	8 15	8 30	9 15	10 35	11 05	11 45
Ar ALBANY	10 47	11 45	1 00	3 25	3 35	6 21	6 45	8 00	A 9 05	9 38		11 27		1 41		
Ar SYRACUSE	2 00	2 30			6 40	9 20	9 35		11 45		2 06	2 35	2 35		4 18	5 20
Ar ROCHESTER	3 16	3 45			8 18	10 16	10 35		1 02			3 53			5 48	6 58
Ar BUFFALO	4 40	4 55			9 40	11 29	11 48		2 15		4 25	5 15	5 00		7 15	8 30
	PM	PM		PM	PM	PM	PM		AM		AM	AM	AM		AM	AM

A—Carries only Reserved Pullman Seat Passengers to Albany.   B—On Saturdays Leaves New York 6:45 PM.   R—All Coach and Parlor Seats Reserved.

BUFFALO—ROCHESTER—SYRACUSE—ALBANY—NEW YORK

Eastbound (EASTERN TIME)	HEN- DRICK HUDSON 154 Ex. Sun.	UP- STATE SPL. 138	PACE- MAKER R2	IRO- QUOIS 38	MO- HAWK 40	CHI- CAGOAN 90	LAUREN- TIAN 134	EMPIRE STATE R50	HUDSON EXP. 196 Sun. Only	DE WITT CLINTON 96	EAST- ERNER 74-52	NEW YORK SPL. 44	5th AVE. SPL. 6	CLEVE. LTD. 58 Ex. Sun.	WOLV- ERINE C8	COMM. V'BILT C68	OHIO STATE C16
	AM	AM	AM	AM	AM	AM	PM	PM	PM	PM	PM	PM	PM	PM	AM	AM	AM
Lv BUFFALO		4 39	7 00	9 30	10 40		1 30		3 00	5 10	11 05	11 15	12 19	1 05		1 35
Lv ROCHESTER		5 47	8 09	10 37	11 55		2 38		4 07	6 28	12 15	12 29			3 23	
Lv SYRACUSE		7 02	9 48	11 56	1 33		4 00		5 25	7 53	1 40	1 48				
Lv ALBANY	7 20	9 00	9 43	12 55	2 35	4 29	5 10	6 35	7 00	A 1 05	4 10	4 25		5 55	6 08	6 20
Ar NEW YORK	10 45	12 15	12 40	3 45	5 25	7 25	8 45	9 30	10 30	5 05	7 10	7 20	7 55	8 45	9 00	9 20
	AM	PM	PM	PM	PM	PM	PM	PM	PM	AM	AM	AM	AM	AM	AM	AM

A—On Monday Mornings No. 52 Leaves Albany 12:35 AM.   C—Coach Seats Reserved.   R—All Coach and Parlor Seats Reserved.

CHICAGO—TOLEDO—CLEVELAND

GREAT LAKES 208	5th AVE. SPL. 6	NEW ENG. STATES R28	PACE- MAKER R2	CHI- CAGOAN 90	FOREST CITY 290 Ex. Sat.	READ DOWN	(La Salle St. Station)	READ UP	PACE- MAKER C1		CHI- CAGOAN 59 Ex. Sun.	IRO- QUOIS 35	CHI- CAGOAN 29 Sun.Only	WEST- ERNER 73	FOREST CITY 89
AM	PM	PM	PM	PM	PM				AM	201	PM	PM	PM	PM	AM
8 45	12 01	2 20	6 20	11 00	11 10		Lv CHICAGO...(C.T.) Ar		7 40	12 15	2 50	5 15	4 15	10 30	7 15
1 57	5 03	7 16	11 17	3 55	4 30		Ar TOLEDO....(E.T.) Lv		4 33	8 45	11 38	2 12	1 10	7 07	3 10
4 12	7 02	9 13		5 52	7 30		Ar CLEVELAND(E.T.) Ar				9 28	12 13	11 09	4 55	12 45
PM	PM	PM		PM	PM				AM	AM	AM	AM	AM	PM	AM

C—Coach Seats Reserved.   R—All Coach and Parlor Seats Reserved.

☞ For complete schedules and intermediate service see condensed and detail tables immediately following.

CHICAGO—DETROIT

MERCURY R376	N.Y. SPL. 44	WOLV- ERINE D8	TWI- LIGHT R30	NIA- GARA 358	MOTOR CITY 316	READ DOWN	(Central Station)	READ UP	NORTH SHORE 39	WOV- ERINE A17	MER- CURY R376	MICH- IGAN 355	TWI- LIGHT R31	MOTOR CITY 315
AM	AM	PM	PM	PM	PM				AM	AM	PM	PM	PM	AM
8 30	10 00	1 55	4 10	7 50	11 59	D	Lv CHICAGO...(C.T.) Ar	U	8 10	11 50	12 50	4 30	9 00	7 20
2 45	5 10	8 05	10 20	2 30	7 45	O W N	Ar DETROIT...(E.T.) Lv	P	3 35	7 30	8 30	12 05	4 45	11 59
PM	PM	PM	PM	AM	AM				AM	AM	PM	PM	PM	AM

A—Arrives LaSalle St. Station.   D—Departs from LaSalle St. Station.   R—All Coach and Parlor Car Seats Reserved.

CHICAGO—INDIAN- APOLIS—CINCINNATI

(Central Station)	CINTI. SPL. 416	CAR. SPL. 406	RILEY R4	ROYAL PALM 438- 410
	AM	PM	PM	PM
Lv CHICAGO......(C.T.)	9 40	1 15	4 20	11 00
Ar INDIANAPOLIS (C.T.)	1 45	6 15	7 50	3 33
Ar CINCINNATI...(E.T.)	5 35	9 00	11 00	7 30
	PM	PM		AM

CLEVELAND—COLUMBUS—SPRINGFIELD— DAYTON—CINCINNATI

XPLOR- ER 423	CINTI. SPL. 433	MER- CURY 401	CAP'L. SPL. 445 Ex. Sat.	MID- NIGHT SPL. 417	READ DOWN	(EASTERN TIME)	READ UP	CAP'L. SPL. 444 Ex. Sun.	MER- CURY 402	CLEVE. SPL. 422	XPLOR- ER 424	NIGHT SPL. 442
AM	PM	PM	PM	PM				AM	PM	PM	PM	AM
8 00	12 35	5 00	7 00	11 59	D	Lv CLEVELAND..... Ar	U	11 00	3 05	6 05	9 05	5 45
10 32	3 42	7 38	10 20	3 01	O	Ar COLUMBUS..... Lv	P	7 50	11 50	3 22	6 20	2 35
11 33	5 05	8 43		4 39	W N	Lv SPRINGFIELD... Lv			10 45	2 25	6 25	1 13
12 14	5 51	9 24		5 34		Lv DAYTON...... Lv			10 05	1 47	4 47	12 28
1 30	7 10	10 40		7 00		Ar CINCINNATI..... Lv			8 45	12 30	3 35	11 00
PM	PM	PM		AM				AM	AM	PM	PM

(Central Station)	RILEY R3	CHGO. SPL. 415	SYCA- MORE 405	ROYAL PALM 443- 437
	AM	AM	PM	PM
Lv CINCINNATI...(E.T.)	8 15	11 35	4 10	11 15
Lv INDIANAPOLIS (C.T.)	9 24	1 00	6 35	1 00
Ar CHICAGO......(C.T.)	1 15	5 55	9 30	5 30
	PM	PM	PM	PM

R—All Coach and Parlor Seats Reserved.

The quick reference timetables from October 1956 leaves one with the impression of a sophisticated operation.

tors at those same intermediate points, dispatchers whose job it was to ensure that the train's safe and timely passage over his territory ("his") because the railroad was male dominated), locomotive and car maintenance personnel from the mechanical department and it becomes apparent that it took a lot of people supported by a highly sophisticated and coordinated organizational structure to deliver a train and its services.

Combining trains from one point to another could save the labor costs of about 40 people—a considerable sum. This required an ever-watchful eye on operations and passenger counts. The railroad's goal was to provide a profitable service which would attract enough people to maintain it. Once the numbers of passengers began to fall, the railroad had to be in a position to react quickly to the drop in an attempt to regain passengers by adjusting schedules or dropping costly services.

Normally, lounge and dining car operations lost money but it was an important service which was deemed essential and one of the attractions of the passenger business. Many of America's passenger trains were well known for the cuisine offered in their dining cars, for example, fresh trout, filet mignon, a particular breakfast omelet, etc. To serve this delicious fare in an atmosphere of elegance required the staff to prepare it, and to serve it, and a dining car department with the knowledge of how to make it worthy of a first-class operation.

A passenger would sit down to a meal at a table covered with white linen with NYC insignia woven in the middle, set with silver-plated utensils embossed with NYC initials, initialed glassware, specially designed and marked china and linen napkins, also woven with the railroad's insignia. Freshly cut flowers were arranged in a small silver-plated vase with silver-plated creamer, teapot and glass water carafe filling out the table's setting. Meanwhile, outside, the country flew by in all types of weather, while inside, comfortably seated and attended, one ordered the Lobster á la Newburg, the *spécialité de la maison,* from the specially tailored train's menu. It was simply luxurious.

The staffing requirements necessitated an infrastructure to support the many services. On NYC the dining car staffs, train crews and coach/parlor car attendants were NYC employees. The sleeping car porters were, until 1958, employees of The Pullman Company which was under contract to the railroad to operate the sleeping cars.

As long as the competition remained another railroad, NYC could hold its own. When the competition became the highway, the bus lines, and the subsidized airlines, coupled with the existing burden of terminal costs, taxes, government regulation and labor contract restrictions, the viability of the entire superstructure of passenger services was undermined. The railroad would have to keep

Silver plated salt and pepper shakers, water pitcher and other tableware were standard issue in NYC dining cars The effect of all the silver contrasted against the ivory liner created an effect which was, without doubt, "sinfully opulent."

the services it offered in line with the amount of traffic Services were cut only a little at a time, as one would prune a tree of dead branches, in the hope that the service could be maintained and, it was hoped, grow back.

As moves were made to cut operating costs, particularly in switching, the observation cars were identified a a nuisance and they were the first amenity to go, usually replaced with a lounge car somewhere in the train.

As mentioned earlier, it had been NYC's practice o attempting to maintain the consistent appearance of th train as much as possible, such as keeping the Bude equipment together, the Pullman-Standard two-tone gra consists together, etc. This was not a problem with th *20th Century Limited,* The *Detroiter,* the *Commodor Vanderbilt* or the *Pacemaker,* but as time went on th operating realities took precedence over the aestheti and before long a mix of gray and stainless steel appeared

Generally, how the cars were located in a train was a much a matter of what cars would be shifted in or out e route. If a train was a through limited with both coache and sleepers, usually the coaches would be located u front, dining and lounge cars in the middle followed b the sleepers. This was subject to change as the necess ties of the services demanded. Deadhead cars usuall wound up ahead of the "head end" revenue (mail expres and baggage) cars.

In an attempt to stem the mounting losses in the pas senger trade (which by 1957 would reach over 52 millio dollars a year), NYC boldly decided to try out two expe imental trains in 1956, prompted by then Chairma Robert R. Young. These came from General Motors/Electr

Motive Division (EMD) and the collaboration of Pullman-Standard and Baldwin-Lima-Hamilton and were designed to be lightweight, swift and low cost. It was intended that these trains (*Aerotrain* and *Xplorer*) capture the public's attention and a lot of publicity heralded their anticipated arrival. They were touted as, "The Trains of the Future" and embodied Young's dreams of reviving passenger train travel.

Unfortunately, the two considerations ignored by the designers of the *Aerotrain* and *Xplorer* were comfort and reliability. The *Xplorer* train set was plagued by mechanical problems, mostly the transmission in the Baldwin locomotive. It often failed en route. While introduced in July 1956 as trains 423 and 424 between Cleveland and Cincinnati, it was quietly withdrawn as problems continued, running in service for just over a year, often with a standard E7 or E8 as power.

The *Aerotrain* was scheduled to begin service in 1956 between Chicago and Detroit on "April 29 to July 28 inclusive, unless sooner changed or extended." It didn't last (because of its rough riding qualities) and was eventually sold to NYC's neighbor at La Salle Street, the Rock Island.

In 1958, the handwriting was on the wall as many social changes were occurring in the country. The automobile was becoming a long distance carrier offering economical and convenient service anywhere. The federal government was helping finance a system of interstate highways for the cars to travel on at high speed. Planes offered service to most cities in a fraction of the time if not cost.

The public was willing to forego the amenities of long distance travel. Comfort was sacrificed for convenience and soon Americans en masse would settle for the mediocrity of a narrow seat and precooked meals. Time, more than ever before, became the essence of travel.

The traveling public—businessmen in suits, ladies in dresses and their families—who before traveled trains for both business and pleasure began to seek other modes in exclusion of the trains. Those who would remain loyal were those who liked train travel or who simply would not fly.

At this time (1958), NYC took over operation of its sleeping cars from The Pullman Company, the cars themselves having been bought (as opposed to leased) from Pullman in 1948. The Pullman name in the cars' corners slowly disappeared and they had their NYC assigned numbers applied under the cars' name as they were shopped.

Coincident with operational transfer, NYC sought to recapture some of its investment in light of declining traffic, and starting in 1958 began selling much of its Great Steel Fleet equipment (in August 1956 NYC had already put up for sale the majority of its passenger stations). The first cars to go were the oldest (from 1938-41) sold to other railroads, mostly in Mexico and Canada and later to the circus.

By 1958, the competition to the Great Steel Fleet was not only the Pennsylvania's fleet of trains, but a societal metamorphosis brought about by progress. For the next 12 years America's passenger trains, with only a few exceptions, were on a schedule of self-destruction.

The early 1960s were the twilight years of the Great Steel Fleet. Even with the cutting of costs, however, NYC

The *Aerotrain* approaches East Cleveland during a press run on a cold and gloomy January 18, 1956.

H. H. Harwood Jr.

Robert R. Young

Robert Young was the visionary chairman of the board of the Chesapeake and Ohio Railway who began a six-year fight for control of the NYC beginning in 1948. He was an articulate and enthusiastic promoter of rail passenger service who combined his Wall Street financing expertise and flamboyance to wage an acrimonious battle resulting in the achievement of his goal in mid-1954 when he became chairman of the board of NYC.

Before gaining control of NYC, he conducted a widely publicized attack on what he considered to be the highly conservative approach of railroad management in light of the evolving conditions in American transportation. He was a champion of new ideas, feeling that the railroads were at a disadvantage in the postwar era. Young championed passenger service, and while he sought innovations in freight service, passenger transportation was his main focus of attention.

C&O Historical Society

While the C&O was not a high-volume passenger carrier, he tried to introduce his revolutionary ideas while he was its chairman. His reforms were short-lived, primarily because C&O didn't have the passenger base to support them. His pet project, "Train X," was to achieve high speeds on existing roadbeds through the use of short, low center of gravity, lightweight cars which, while never seeing service on C&O, did materialize briefly on NYC as *Xplorer*.

When Young came to the NYC in 1954, the nation's transportation framework had indeed changed and competition from trucks and the airlines were challenging his new acquisition. NYC was a troubled railroad by the time Young became its board chairman. To help rescue NYC, he hired a talented executive who had saved the Denver & Rio Grande Western from bankruptcy—Alfred Perlman.

President Perlman quickly set to work reorganizing NYC's moneymaker, its freight operations. He also began talks with the Pennsylvania Railroad about a merger of the two rivals.

Tragically, in late January 1958, Robert Young committed suicide and Alfred Perlman quickly turned his attention to NYC's hemorrhaging passenger service. By April, the major restructuring of the NYC's passenger service began.

In 1961, the ICC approved the merger of the New York Central and Pennsylvania Railroads. It would be another seven years before all the court challenges could be resolved and the new company, Penn Central, would come to symbolize the low point in the history of America's railroads.

The new creation would prove to be too large to manage efficiently. To make matters worse, the two managements were antagonistic toward each other; their styles of administration were difficult to reconcile; locomotives had differing signal, brake, and multiple engine control connection locations; the computer systems were incompatible and the two railroads merged without enough cash in the bank to see them through the initial phases of the merger. In short, confusion reigned supreme and the venture lost money from the first day of operation.

The new railroad collapsed into bankruptcy in 1970 and would emerge combined with other bankrupt northeast railroads in April 1976 as the Consolidated Rail Corporation, or Conrail. Robert R. Young would not have been pleased.

The *Aerotrain* approaches East Cleveland in January, 1956. Its rough ride could not be overcome and while innovative, that in itself was not enough for the railroad to pursue the experiment.

H. H. Harwood Jr.

strove to maintain its high standards of operation, although some of its grander terminals felt the cuts in expenses more severely through reduced maintenance.

Accelerating the demise of the passenger train was the loss of the U.S. Mail contracts at the instigation of Postmaster General Lawrence O'Brien in the mid-1960s. With air travel quickly becoming cost effective and less time consuming, the decision was made to phase out the Railway Post Office and move sealed pouch mail contracts to trucks and first-class mail to the air.

Up to this juncture, when the railroads lost money on a train, sometimes the deficit was made up through freight or mail revenues. Occasionally, the RPO and mail/express contracts reduced the operating costs of the train, even though they also incurred their own operating costs. In an ironic twist, history would repeat itself in the age of Amtrak. (It would be the mail contracts that would help sustain the national passenger rail network in the 1990s.)

With the loss of these contracts, which ultimately affected the (collectively railroad-owned) Railway Express Agency as well, a blow was struck to NYC's revenue base. This singular move would add urgency to the need to drastically reduce operating costs as the passenger train deficits further eroded the railroad's profits and imperiled its very existence. It was a downward spiral which threatened to turn into a tail spin.

Ultimately, it was "progress," state and federal government regulation, and out-dated work rules which caught up with the passenger train and left it behind. As difficult as it may have seemed, passenger train travel didn't have a future and no railroad could afford further expenses or investments in new equipment.

The New York Central issued its last timetable on December 3, 1967. Two months later the proud railroad and its Great Steel Fleet were memories.

New York Central Railroad Passengers Carried and Passenger-miles 1948-1967		
1948	68,822,445	5,526,449,260
1949	61,618,247	4,649,869,910
1950	46,627,062	3,928,972,714
1951	46,741,774	4,046,196,104
1952	45,109,107	3,958,765,329
1953	44,193,462	3,731,316,560
1954	43,593,216	3,521,180,608
1955	43,432,503	3,379,528,082
1956	43,459,232	3,196,813,539
1957	40,026,332	2,693,689,945
1958	37,177,714	2,272,826,029
1959	32,456,208	1,975,983,215
1960	30,451,557	1,796,665,005
1961	27,711,299	1,531,040,077
1962	27,625,338	1,489,650,200
1963	25,138,208	1,300,371,793
1964	26,423,711	1,342,831,577
1965	24,790,153	1,207,014,604
1966	25,572,716	1,127,834,874
1967	24,663,917	939,378,514

Reported in Railroad Annual Report Form R-1, published in Transport Statistics in the United States, prepared by the Interstate Commerce Commission, Office of Economic and Environmental Analysis

Admittedly, by 1967, the Great Steel Fleet had long lost its luster and what was left could hardly be termed, "great," and little of it remained.

The postwar Great Steel Fleet, riding a tide of optimism in 1948, flourished in the 1950s. While it lingered in spirit, its demise can be traced to as early as 1949. It survives as a distant memory today and the photographs remain as a testament to a more civilized age when service incorporated style, courtesy, and comfort—not just getting there. Indeed, when one traveled the trains of the Great Steel Fleet, "getting there was half the fun."

"Secondary trains" was a term used to describe those trains of the fleet which were the workhorses and of lesser stature than the limiteds. They were assigned secondary power, such as these two GP7s pulling a mix of ACF and Pullman-Standard streamline and lightweight equipment in this circa 1950 view.

Author's Collection

Pausing at East Cleveland the westbound *Aerotrain* press run awaits the conductor's highball. That observation car looks like the rear of a '56 Cadillac. Somehow the standard coupler under the flashing lights looks out of place. Note the letters "GM" between the lights. One of the Budd built baggage dormitory cars is on the adjacent track on the rear of a westbound train.

Not as elegant as the lightning stripe scheme, the "cigar band" was less expensive to apply. NYC experimented with a variety of paint schemes before settling on this with dark grey with white lettering. This is Train No. 201 at South Bend, Indiana on June 1, 1965.

Collection of Louis A. Marre

Image

Both the 1938 and 1948 *20th Century Limiteds* were designed by Henry Dreyfuss—one of America's most distinguished industrial designers. The Hudson-type locomotives for the 1938 Century sported a suspended shroud, which was likewise designed by Dreyfuss, and became the symbol by which the 20th Century Limited was recognized by millions.

By 1948, the *20th Century Limited* was being pulled by either steam or diesel locomotives, but the steam locomotives were no longer outfitted in the famous and distinctive Dreyfuss-styled shroud. The "lightning stripe" scheme which adorned the new passenger diesels was handsome and striking in appearance, nevertheless.

In 1953, New York Central decided to dress up the locomotives which were pulling the trains of the 1948 Great Steel Fleet. Silver paint was applied to the utilitarian black trucks of the passenger diesels which added another dimension of "class" to the new "thoroughbreds."

The silver appearance of the trucks proved difficult to keep clean and in 1957, as the railroad sought to reduce maintenance costs, the trucks were either painted black during regular shopping or were simply allowed to be covered by dirt and grime.

Coincident with the implementation of the "trains of the future," (*Aerotrain* and *Xplorer*) the NYC redesigned the familiar New York Central System oval herald to reflect the image change in 1956. "Central" was written in script and "System" was replaced by horizontal lines. This herald appeared on some locomotives, most notably on E8 4044 in Alfred Hitchcock's, *North by Northwest*, but it wasn't widely applied and in many cases was removed and replaced with its forerunner. (In October 1959 an updated revised, slimmer Form 1001 appeared with the new and last redesigned New York Central herald which would serve until the Penn Central merger.)

With the inauguration of the Young-Perlman era, the NYC became the "Road to the Future" and the railroad again made moves to cut costs in the high maintenance color scheme of their passenger locomotive fleet.

Several experimental paint schemes were tried in 1960, 1961, and 1962 before the final version of the easier-to-maintain "cigar band" scheme replaced the appealing lightning stripes of 1948. This consisted of a dark gray engine with a single white band which ran lengthwise around the engine. Interestingly enough, one locomotive which had an experimental scheme applied to it, E8 No. 4056, had the insignia and lightning stripes of 1948 reapplied.

In 1963, NYC made its decision and the cigar band scheme became the standard for the aging locomotives.

Collection of Louis A. Marre

No. 4006 off of a football special at Notre Dame (South Bend) wears the "script" herald with lightning stripes on October 3, 1958. The silver painted trucks still show up well in this view. Note the Hancock air whistle on 4006.

Terminal operations were complex. In this view of Cincinnati Union Terminal, we are looking south at the passenger terminal in the distance; mail and express operations to the top left center; and the coach yard where cars from the Southern, C&O and NYC are being serviced. In the foreground the *Cincinnati Mercury* (Cincinnati-Cleveland) is being made up with cars from the original train, a standard heavyweight buffet-lounge car and two Budd *Harbor* series 22 Roomette sleepers acting as parlor cars. This Wallace Abbey photo was made on September 24, 1952. Today, Norfolk Southern's piggyback operations occupies this same site.

Courtesy Trains Magazine

THE ACCOMMODATIONS

In 1948, there were two ways to travel on a train: in a coach (or parlor car seat) or in a sleeping car. While coaches were rather straightforward in design, the sleeping cars offered the traveler a choice of accommodations. NYC ordered its fleet of sleeping cars from Pullman-Standard and Budd. These were staffed through a contractual agreement with The Pullman Company.

The Pullman Company and Pullman-Standard Car Manufacturing Company were two separate entities, commonly referred to as "Pullman." Pullman-Standard built all types of railroad cars, both freight and passenger. The Pullman Company provided the staff and support services to operate the cars in train service on the railroads throughout the United States and Mexico.

The Pullman-Standard Car Manufacturing Company, along with the Edward G. Budd Manufacturing Company, or "Budd," designed passenger equipment in accordance with specifications provided to them from the various railroads with a variety of floor plans suited for each type of train service.

In the pre-streamline era, the sleeping arrangements in the standard cars were limited to "sections ('sec.')" containing two sofa seats facing each other which would be converted into a lower berth with an upper berth lowered from the car wall and curtains hung to offer some privacy; compartments ("comp.") for two persons sequestered from the section portion of the car; bedrooms ("bdrm.") usually for two persons but smaller than a compartment; and drawing rooms ("D.R.") for two or three persons which were much larger with sofas. Room arrangements depended upon the floor plan, of which there were many.

With the debut of the all-room streamlined cars, and in particular the streamlined cars for the *20th Century Limited*, the patron was offered a new type of accommodation for those traveling alone—the roomette. This was a self-contained room offering toilet and washstand, small sofa, and a bed which folded out of the wall behind the sofa. The room measured roughly 6-1/2 feet x 3 feet.

A large mirror was provided on the opposite wall with luggage storage overhead. Next to the doorway and slightly above was the shoe locker which could be accessed from the aisle by the porter who would shine the shoes over night if the patron so desired. A small closet was provided next to the sofa and there was a bank of switches by the door so the heat, air conditioning, lights, and fan could be controlled, along with a call button to summon the porter.

Important Notices

New York Central System passenger trains are frequently operated in two or more sections. It is therefore necessary that friends who expect to wire you en route, or meet you at stations, should know the *number or name of your train*. When more than one section of a train is operated, it frequently happens that only the regular section will make all of the advertised stops. Passengers expecting others to accompany them part of the journey, or to join them en route, are requested to inquire at starting point what stops will be made.

AIR-CONDITIONED TRAINS AND INDIVIDUAL SEAT COACHES—Air-conditioned equipment and individual seat coaches have been assigned to regular sections of certain trains. Every effort will be made to provide this equipment but the right is reserved to employ non-air-conditioned cars and non-individual-seat coaches in such trains as may be necessitated by volume of traffic or operating contingencies.

Special Service Charges on Trains Nos. 26 and 25
"Twentieth Century Limited"
Subject to Federal Tax

BETWEEN	AND	
	Chicago	Englewood
Harmon	4.85	4.85
New York	5.00	5.00

HOW TO PHONE PASSENGERS ABOARD THE CENTURY

Ring Long Distance. Ask to make a person to person call to your party on The Twentieth Century Limited. Just give the name and specify Eastbound or Westbound. Westbound, telephone between 6:00 PM and 11:00 PM; Eastbound, from early morning until arrival at Grand Central Terminal at 9:30 AM. (Eastern Standard time in all cases.)

Limited Train Features

Special service features are provided on limited trains as follows
Nos. 25 and 26—Twentieth Century Limited.
Club-Lounge Car—Barber, Secretary, Valet, Shower Bath, Radio—Telephone, Magazines, Newspapers, Stationery.
Observation Car—Telephone at Terminals, Lounge, Radio, Magazines, Newspapers, Stationery.

SPECIAL SERVICE CHARGES FOR PASSENGERS OCCUPYING RESERVED COACH SEATS
ON

"THE JAMES WHITCOMB RILEY", Cincinnati, Ohio — Chicago, Ill.
"THE TWILIGHT LIMITED", Chicago, Ill. — Detroit, Mich.
"THE CHICAGO MERCURY", Chicago, Ill. — Detroit, Mich.
"THE CLEVELAND MERCURY", Detroit, Mich. — Cleveland, Ohio
"THE PACEMAKER", Chicago, Ill. — New York, N. Y.
"NEW ENGLAND STATES", Chicago, Ill. — Boston, Mass.
"EMPIRE STATE EXPRESS" { New York, N. Y. — Cleveland, Ohio
{ Detroit, Mich.

Where the distance between points traveled is	Special Service Charge will be:	Federal Tax
1 to 150 miles	$ .25	$ .04
151 to 350 miles	.50	.08
351 to 600 miles	.75	.11
601 miles or over	1.00	.15

"NEW ROYAL PALM", Detroit, Mich.—Miami, Fla.
Special Service Charge to all points beyond Cincinnati, O.,—$1.00 (except between certain points 75c).

REDEMPTION OF SPECIAL SERVICE CHARGE TICKETS COVERING RESERVED COACH SEATS

Tickets sold prior to date of departure redeemable only if space is released on or before day prior to date of departure.
Tickets sold on date of departure redeemable only if space is released at least three hours prior to departure of train.

National Travelers Aid Society

TRAVELERS AID workers are at many of the railroad stations ready to assist inexperienced and unprotected travelers and all those in trouble away from home. Look for the TRAVELERS AID lamp, or ask station personnel where to find TRAVELERS AID.

Bus Service to and from Central Terminal, Buffalo

Frequent bus service is provided to and from New York Central Terminal at Buffalo and the hotels and downtown district.
Fare fifteen cents. Free transfers between all local bus lines.
Buses arrive at and leave from the Upper Level of Central Terminal. No stairs to climb.

Chautauqua on Lake Chautauqua

Passengers for Chautauqua Institution on Lake Chautauqua in Western New York, famous educational, religious music and cultural center, may stop over at Westfield, N. Y., on New York Central main line and take the short motor coach trip of ten miles via Central Greyhound Lines.
TRAVELERS' CHEQUES—American Express Travelers' Cheques are on sale at principal ticket offices, offering a further convenience to patrons.

From a 1950 Form 1001. A glance at the important notices is a snapshot of the era - i.e. extra sections of a train, air conditioned trains (not all trains had a/c), the special service charges and the ever-present tax.

PULLMAN, COACH AND DINING CAR SERVICE
TRAINS NOT SHOWN CARRY COACHES ONLY
Regularly assigned cars are air-conditioned

WESTBOUND

No. 1—THE PACEMAKER—DAILY—STREAMLINER
ALL COACH SEATS RESERVED—PORTER SERVICE

Observation Lounge Coach (Beverages)
  New York to Chicago
Dining Service
Reclining Seat Coaches
  New York to Chicago

No. 3—THE JAMES WHITCOMB RILEY—DAILY STREAMLINER
ALL COACH SEATS RESERVED—PORTER SERVICE

Sleeping Car
  Asheville, N. C. to Chicago (10 Roomette-6 Double Bedroom)—*From Sou. Ry. No. 28 at Cincinnati*
Dining Service
Observation Lounge Coach (Beverages)
  Cincinnati to Chicago
Reclining Seat Coaches
  Cincinnati to Chicago

No. 5—DAILY

Lounge Sleeping Car
  Buffalo to Chicago (6 Double Bedroom-Buffet)
  Buffet Breakfast Service into Chicago
Sleeping Cars
  Buffalo to St. Louis, Ex. Sat. (10 Roomette-6 Double Bedroom)—*In No. 41 from Cleveland*
  Buffalo to Chicago (10 Roomette-5 Double Bedroom)—*Will not run Sept. 2*
  Buffalo to Cincinnati, Ex. Sat. (10 Roomette-5 Double Bedroom)—*In No. 417 from Cleveland*
  Toledo to Chicago, Ex. Sat. Night-Sun. Morn. (22 Roomette) *Will not run a.m. of Sept. 3*
Coaches
  Buffalo to Chicago

No. 11—SOUTHWESTERN LIMITED—DAILY STREAMLINER

Lounge Sleeping Car
  New York to St. Louis (6 Double Bedroom-Beverages)—*From No. 19-11 at Cleveland*
Sleeping Cars
  New York to St. Louis (10 Roomette-6 Double Bedroom)—*Two—From No. 19-11 at Cleveland*
  Boston to St. Louis (10 Roomette-6 Double Bedroom)—*From No. 19-11 at Cleveland*
  Richmond, Va. to St. Louis (10 Roomette-6 Double Bedroom)—*From C. & O. No. 41-1 at Cincinnati, No. 415 at Indianapolis*
Dining Service
  New York to Albany
  Boston to Albany—Diner Lounge
  Cleveland to St. Louis
Coaches
  New York to St. Louis (Reclining Seat)—*From No. 19-11 at Cleveland*
  Boston to Albany
  Cincinnati to St. Louis—*From No. 415 at Indianapolis*

No. 15—OHIO STATE LIMITED—DAILY STREAMLINER

Sleeping Cars
  New York to Cincinnati (10 Roomette-6 Double Bedroom)—Two
  New York to Cincinnati (22 Roomette)
  New York to Columbus (10 Roomette-6 Double Bedroom)
  New York to Cincinnati (10 Roomette-6 Double Bedroom)—*From No. 49 at Buffalo (Effective Sept. 10 operates in No. 141 New York to Buffalo)*
  Boston to Cincinnati (10 Roomette-6 Double Bedroom)—*From No. 49 at Buffalo (Effective Sept. 10 operates in No. 49 to Albany—No. 141 to Buffalo)*
  Buffalo to Cincinnati (22 Roomette)
  New York to Chicago (10 Roomette-6 Double Bedroom)—*Two—In No. 27 from Buffalo*
Dining Service
Lounge Car (Beverages)
  New York to Cincinnati
Coaches
  New York to Cincinnati (Reclining Seat)

No. 17—THE WOLVERINE—DAILY
(ARRIVES AT LA SALLE ST. STATION)

Lounge Sleeping Car
  New York to Chicago (6 Double Bedroom-Beverages)
  Boston to Detroit, Sat. only (6 Double Bedroom-Beverages)—*From No. 33 at Buffalo Sunday mornings*
Sleeping Cars
  New York to Los Angeles (10 Roomette-6 Double Bedroom)—*In Milwaukee-U. P. No. 103 from Chicago*
  New York to Chicago (10 Roomette-6 Double Bedroom)—Two
  New York to Detroit, Sat. only (10 Roomette-6 Double Bedroom)
  New York to Detroit, Sat. only (12 Double Bedroom)
  New York to Jackson (10 Roomette-5 Double Bedroom)
  Boston to Chicago (10 Roomette-6 Double Bedroom)—*From No. 33 at Buffalo*
  Buffalo to Detroit, Ex. Sat. Night-Sun. Morn. (22 Roomette)
Dining Service
Lounge Coach (Beverages)
  New York to Chicago
Coaches
  New York to Chicago (Reclining Seat)

No. 19—LAKE SHORE LIMITED—DAILY
For New York and Boston-St. Louis equipment
See No. 11—Southwestern Limited

Sleeping Cars
  New York to Toledo (10 Roomette-6 Double Bedroom)—*In No. 75-760 from Cleveland*
  Boston to Toledo (22 Roomette)—*In No. 75-760 from Cleveland*
  Boston to Cleveland, Ex. Sat. (10 Roomette-6 Double Bedroom)—*In No. 57 from Albany. Will not run Sept. 2*
  Boston to Toronto (10 Roomette-6 Double Bedroom—*In No. 57-21 from Albany to No. 371 at Buffalo*
  Toronto to Cleveland, Sat. only (22 Roomette)—*From No. 382 at Buffalo. Will also run Sept. 2*
Dining Service
  New York to Albany
  Boston to Albany—Diner Lounge
Coaches
  New York to Cleveland (Reclining Seats)
  Boston to Albany

No. 21—THE NORTH STAR—SAT. ONLY
Will also run Sept. 2

Lounge Sleeping Car
  New York to Lake Placid (6 Double Bedroom-Buffet)
  Buffet Breakfast Service into Lake Placid
  New York to Cleveland (6 Double Bedroom-Buffet)
Sleeping Cars
  New York to Toronto (10 Roomette-6 Double Bedroom)—Two—*In No. 371 from Buffalo*
  New York to Lake Placid (8 Sec.-D.R.-3 Double Bedroom)—*In Adk. Div. No. 5 from Utica*
  Boston to Toronto (10 Roomette-6 Double Bedroom)—*From No. 19-11 at Albany to No. 371 at Buffalo*
  New York to Cleveland (10 Roomette-6 Double Bedroom)
  New York to Plattsburg (8 Sec.-5 Double Bedroom)—*In D. & H. No. 7 from Albany*
Dining Service (Thrift Grill)
  Buffalo to Cleveland
Coaches
  New York to Cleveland
  New York to Toronto—*In No. 371 from Buffalo*

No. 23—NORTH SHORE LIMITED—SUN. ONLY
See No. 39

No. 25—TWENTIETH CENTURY LIMITED—EX. SAT. STREAMLINER
Will not run Sept. 2
New York to Los Angeles cars will operate in Train 67 on Saturdays and on above dates
For special service features and charges see page 47

Observation Lounge Sleeping Car
  New York to Chicago (5 Double Bedroom-Beverages)
Club Lounge Car (Beverages)
  New York to Chicago
Sleeping Cars
  New York to Los Angeles (4 Comp.-4 Double Bedroom-2 D.R.)—*In Santa Fe No. 17 from Chicago*
  New York to Los Angeles (10 Roomette-6 Double Bedroom)—*In Santa Fe No. 17 from Chicago*
  New York to Chicago (4 Comp.-4 Double Bedroom-2 D.R.)
  New York to Chicago (12 Double Bedroom)—Four
  New York to Chicago (10 Roomette-6 Double Bedroom)—Two
Dining Service
Pullman Cars only; no coach passengers carried

No. 27—NEW ENGLAND STATES—DAILY STREAMLINER

Sleeping Cars
  Boston to Chicago (10 Roomette-6 Dbl. Bedroom)—Four
  Albany to Chicago (10 Roomette-6 Double Bedroom)—Two
  Albany to Chicago (22 Roomette)
  New York to Chicago (10 Roomette-6 Double Bedroom)—Two—*From No. 15 at Buffalo*
  Buffalo to Chicago (10 Roomette-6 Double Bedroom)
Dining Service
Lounge Car (Beverages)
  Boston to Chicago
Reclining Seat Coaches—Porter Service
  Boston to Chicago—All seats Reserved

No. 29—THE CHICAGOAN—SAT. ONLY
Will also run Sept. 2

Lounge Sleeping Cars
  New York to Chicago (6 Double Bedroom-Buffet)
Sleeping Cars
  New York to Chicago (10 Roomette-6 Double Bedroom)
  New York to Chicago (10 Roomette-5 Dbl. Bedroom)
  New York to Cleveland (10 Roomette-6 Double Bedroom)
  New York to Buffalo (10 Roomette-6 Double Bedroom)
  New York to Syracuse (10 Roomette-6 Double Bedroom)
  New York to Rochester (10 Roomette-6 Double Bedroom)
  New York to Niagara Falls (10 Roomette-5 Double Bedroom)—*In 217 from Buffalo*
  New York to Toronto (10 Roomette-6 Double Bedroom)—*In No. 377 from Buffalo*
Dining Service
  Buffalo to Chicago
Coaches
  New York to Chicago (Reclining Seat)

The premier trains of the Great Steel Fleet were highlighted in the consist section of the timetable with the word "streamliner." This chart from the July 1956 timetable shows the wide variety of sleeping car movements.

On the Level you can sleep...

...on New York Central's gentle Water Level Route!

With the introduction of the 1948 sleeping cars, Pullman-Standard, Budd and NYC offered the latest in sleeping car accommodations, modern bedrooms and roomettes with some of the refurbished pre-war cars which contained compartments and drawing rooms. The Great Steel Fleet of 1948 boasted a sleeping car service which was second to none.

The last type of accommodation introduced to the patrons of NYC was in 1959 when the railroad leased from Budd four 24-roomette/8-double bedroom "sleepercoaches," known on some other railroads as "slumbercoaches." The idea was to accommodate as many persons in a car as possible in order to get a higher rate of return per car, with patrons served by one porter. A sleepercoach could accommodate forty persons as compared to twenty-two persons in a modern 10-roomette/6-double bedroom car.

Similar cars had been in service on the Burlington Route's *Denver Zephyr* since 1956 and had not only proven to be popular but also a financial success. By 1959, NYC was looking for another way to keep passengers on its trains and still earn a modest profit.

The duplex roomettes were smaller than a Pullman-Standard or Budd roomette (the latter

The *20th Century* is leaving New York on a cold winter's night in 1963. Visible are a Budd coach, a rebuilt 22 roomette sleepercoach, grill diner and two 24-8 sleepercoaches.

NYC Photo, J. W. Swanberg Collection

two being of the same dimensions) and staggered, an upper and lower with tight overhead clearance and a small bed which came out from ahead and behind the small seat. When the two halves were lowered, rectangular mattresses on each half were then overlaid by an inch thick 6 foot long mattress, 2 feet wide to bridge the minuscule gap in the middle, with bedding all made as it unfolded from one end. Washstand and toilet were located next to the seat on the aisle side. The lower roomette

was quite claustrophobic with the two ends of the upper's bed on either side intruding into the small cubicle.

The sleepercoach bedrooms were actually the same dimensions as a Pullman/Budd roomette, only with two seats facing each other and toilet and washstand next to the sliding door in the corner. A roomette for one person is comfortable—a roomette for two is a tight fit. Like the roomette, the bedroom did offer privacy. Unlike the

SEE FOR YOURSELF THE LUXURIES OF TRAIN TRAVEL
SMART ACCOMMODATIONS FOR EVERY BUDGET AND NEED

INDIVIDUAL RECLINING COACH SEATS . . . comfortable as your favorite easy chair and built to tilt up for reading or window-gazing, back for lazing . . . way back for napping.

UPPER AND LOWER BERTHS . . . have individually controlled reading lights and ventilation, deep-cushioned mattresses, clothes hangers, call bell, adjustable seats for day.

COZY ROOMETTES . . . everything for the individual traveler. Sitting room by day, bedroom by night. Complete toilet and washing facilities, individual temperature controls.

BEDROOMS AND COMPARTMENTS . . . contain two beds, a lower and an upper. Lavatory, wash basin, air-conditioning controls. Compartments are larger and differ from bedrooms in arrangement of beds.

SUITES FOR GROUP TRAVEL . . . are prepared by folding back doors between two adjoining bedrooms. By day a sitting room with divans, movable chairs; by night, four beds. Toilet and washing facilities, temperature controls.

DRAWING ROOMS . . . have three beds — two lower, one upper plus enclosed toilet and washing facilities, individual temperature controls. By day folding chairs and a table may be used. Ideal for the family.

YOUR *Vacation* STARTS WHEN YOU BOARD THE TRAIN

SCENIC WATER LEVEL ROUTE
Your New York Central train between the East and the Midwest follows a smooth, scenic river valley and lake shore route.
The approach to and departure from New York is past the majestic scenery of the broad Hudson River . . . the jutting cliffs of the Palisades, the fabled Washington Irving country and renowned West Point.

roomette, the sleepercoach bedroom contained an upper berth which was lowered from above the window.

The cost for a sleepercoach ticket was slightly higher than that of coach fare and the cars were an instant success. The new economy accommodations would remain popular for as long as the cars were in service.

In time, as the older cars were retired, the roomette and double bedroom arrangements became the standard sleeping accommodations of NYC's passenger fleet. The sleepercoaches, with their smaller accommodations, augmented the sleeping car service and if nothing else, offered the traveler another alternative of affordable passage.

What's New on the Menu?

New "King-Size" diners head New York Central's NEW dining car fleet

Your first taste of dining car hospitality may come with before-dinner refreshments in the lounge. But everywhere on Central you find the same ready service and warm welcome.

Central attraction is that famous New York Central food. Anything from a tempting breakfast to a hearty dinner . . . fresh from the gleaming new stainless-steel kitchen.

STEP THROUGH an electric-eye door into an exciting new mealtime world. Step into a double dining car unit so spacious it includes a separate kitchen car. So luxurious it has its own refreshment lounge with club chairs and wide-view windows.

And these "king-size" dining cars are only the headliners. There are fine new single-unit diners and smart new grill cars, too. A whole new dining car fleet . . . going into service on New York Central's great daily trains.

NEW York Central
The Water Level Route — You Can Sleep

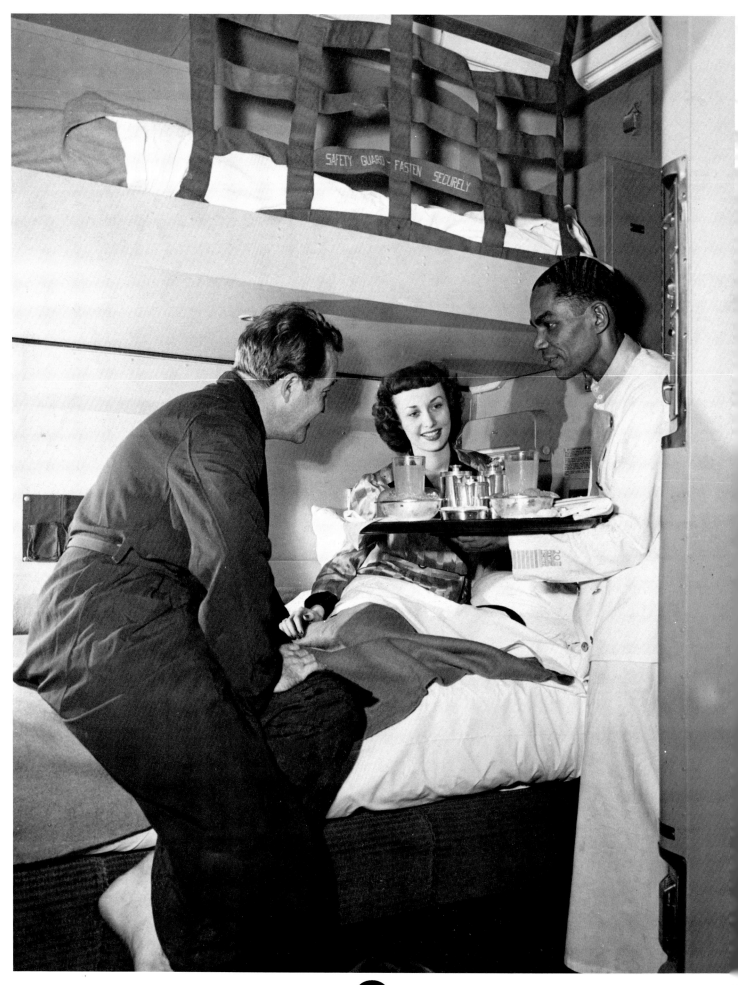

SAFETY GUARD - FASTEN SECURELY

CENTRAL'S ECONOMICAL ALL-ROOM

SLEEPERCOACHES

New York Central's All-Room Sleepercoach fleet serves overnight travellers to or from most principal cities including service on the 20th Century and New England States between Chicago, New York, Boston. Among these cities are Rochester, Buffalo, Erie, Cleveland, Columbus, Springfield, (O.); Dayton, Cincinnati, Detroit.

Next time you plan a trip, be sure to ask your New York Central ticket agent or your travel agent for full details on Sleepercoach service available locally.

Check these convenience and economy features:

- Pay only low coach fare plus modest flat room charge
- Relax in privacy and comfort
- Enjoy Dining and Lounge car service
- Save with Central's Family Fare Plan
- All-weather schedules
- Single or double rooms
- Washstand and toilet in every room
- Special infant accommodations
- Connecting service to the West
- Reduced fares for round trips

PRIVATE BEDROOM with toilet and washstand

Single Room	$ 7.00
Double Room	$12.60

A smooth comfortable ride in a private room enables you to work, read, or relax and watch the countryside whiz by.

Same space as a private bedroom at night, double (as shown above) or single, for peaceful sleep.

At left: A uniformed waiter with a monogrammed sleeve arrives with a late evening repast. Room service was available aboard most trains which had sleepers and dining cars.

At right: A parlor/ observation car offered large, but debatably, comfortable chairs with a view at the rear of the train.

Both: NYC Photo, J. W. Swanberg Collection

From the looks on these faces, this posing assignment was probably not their favorite activity. Perhaps giving them a real dinner in the diner might bring some smiles to their faces.

NYC Photo, J. W. Swanberg Collection

THE CARS

The NYC catered to a great number of business travelers, many of whom traveled with their wives, in addition to persons traveling for vacations and on personal business. Having the ability to offer these persons comfortable lodging, coach seats and the amenities of parlor seats, lounges, and dining cars became one of the most important assets of the Great Steel Fleet of 1948.

Ten years earlier an exciting modern service had been introduced with the inauguration of the streamlined *20th Century Limited*. Additional sleeping and lounge cars had been ordered from Pullman-Standard at the same time to equip other trains, in part, right up to the outbreak of the Second World War. At its end NYC wanted to resume its modernization program.

Four months after the close of World War II, in December 1945, NYC placed passenger car orders with the two largest builders of passenger equipment: Pullman-Standard and Budd. By the time the second streamline *20th Century Limited* was christened (in no less a way than a luxury liner) in September 1948, the railroad had embarked on an ambitious program of streamlining its entire long distance and "world's largest passenger fleet."

The older (eight to ten years old) first generation streamlined cars were refurbished and placed in service with the new equipment. Soon the long distance traveler would find roomettes, bedrooms, in a variety of individually named cars in several new "series" named for the geographical terrain associated with the east-west main line NYC traversed: valleys, rivers, streams, lakes, bays, ports, creeks, brooks and harbors. This was, after all, the "water level route."

The passenger cars of the streamline design quickly replaced the older cars known as "heavyweight" or "standard." Several types of sleeping cars quickly became the gems of the 1948 Great Steel Fleet:

The roomette cars which came in two series: 17- and 18-roomette pre-war *City* series and 22-roomette postwar *Bay* series from Pullman; and 22-roomette *Harbor* series from Budd;

Roomette/double bedroom cars containing 10-roomettes/5-double bedrooms (10-5) prewar *Cascade* cars and 10-roomette/6-double bedroom (10-6) *River* post-war series cars from Pullman; and *Valley* series from Budd;

Bedroom cars containing 13-double bedrooms in the prewar *County* series cars and 12-double bedroom *Port* series post-war cars from Pullman; 4-bedroom/4-compartment/2-drawing room (or 4-4-2) *Imperial* (some later were renamed for bridges) series prewar cars from Pullman; Bedroom/lounge cars: 6-double bedroom/lounge cars in three series, *Falls* (prewar Pullman), *Lake* (post-war Pullman-Standard) and *Stream* from Budd. These often served as parlor cars.

Bedrooms were also contained in the crown jewels of the Great Steel Fleet, the 13 observation cars for the *Commodore Vanderbilt, New England States, Ohio State Limited, Southwestern Limited* and the *20th Century Limited*.

Stainless steel twin-unit dining car sets which contained a lounge in the kitchen car and single unit dining cars provided elegant dining service en route. Buffet/lounge cars from Budd offered additional snack and beverage service to tide over the passenger before

Author's Collection

The Great Steel (coach) Fleet at Pullman-Standard in this 1946 view.

disembarking.

It is true that NYC didn't provide any exotic equipment comparable to the Pennsy's "recreation cars" which were constructed for use in the New York-St. Louis *Jeffersonian* or the dome cars of the western railroads. In fact, even the lounges of the western routes with their popular western motif interiors, such as the "Chuck Wagon" cars on the Burlington's *Denver Zephyr*; "Ranch" cars on the Great Northern's *Empire Builder* or the "Lewis & Clark" lounge on the Northern Pacific's *North Coast Limited* were more aesthetically appealing and unique.

One can only imagine how a "Puritan's Tavern Lounge" on the *New England States* might have been received. Nevertheless, NYC operations were so vast it had to have a fleet which could be as versatile as possible. As a result, it opted for equipment which, while maybe not remarkable and even might today be called "off the shelf," was new and comfortable and was integrated into trains providing exceptionally high-quality service.

The main difference, naturally, lies in the scale of passenger operations. The western roads didn't operate as large a passenger fleet as did NYC and the demands for equipment were therefore limited in scale.

This enormous fleet conveyed the pampered passenger in such comfort and style that it made traveling by train a most pleasurable experience. Whether in a coach or in a compartment, persons would arrive rested, relaxed, and looking forward to another journey aboard the trains of the New York Central.

Mostly Sleepers in N.Y.C.
Order Placed with Budd

Of the 112 cars of stainless-steel construction ordered from the Edward G. Budd Manufacturing Company by the New York Central and announced in the December 15 *Railway Age*, page 1005, approximately 80% will be sleepers with the Budd-originated-and-developed double bedroom and cabin accommodations. Other equipment in the order consists of lounge facilities, observation facilities, diners, combination kitchen and lounge cars and baggage-dormitory cars. Deliveries of these cars, which will be used to make up eight trains, are scheduled to begin in the fall of 1946.

The 112 passenger cars are in addition to an order for 127 on which Budd is now working for the New York Central. The total cost of all of the equipment approximates $22,000,000.

*(Excerpted from Railway Age
December 22, 1945)*

NYC Buys 22 More Trains

Reportedly the largest single order for passenger equipment in the history of American railroading was announced on December 13 by Gustav Metzman, president of the New York Central System. The $34,000,000 order represents 22 luxurious, streamlined sleeping car trains totaling 420 passenger cars. These are in addition to the 300 de luxe passenger cars already under construction for Central's daytime trains. The 720 new cars currently on order are the equivalent of 52 new streamliners and represent a total cost of $56,000,000.

Each one of the sleeping cars will be of the all-room type and will include the latest developments of the car builder's Art Deco single rooms, double bedrooms and deluxe bedroom suite. The new type dining cars, lounges and observation cars have been planned by the Central's engineers and designers in cooperation with the manufacturers' experts in these fields.

Of the new order, 200 cars for sleeping car service will be built by the Pullman-Standard Car Manufacturing Company, Chicago, of high-tensile, low alloy steel, with welded girder construction, and will be painted the famous "Century" two-toned gray; 112 cars of stainless steel will be built by the Edward G. Budd Manufacturing Company; the American Car and Foundry Company will build 108 streamlined baggage, baggage-mail and railway post office cars.

The first of the new sleeping cars employing the most modern ideas in safety, comfort and decoration, are expected to be ready next September. Thereafter, they will come in a steady flow from the manufacturers until completion of the order in March, 1947. As the new equipment is received, it will go into service on the *"Twentieth Century Limited,"* the *"Commodore Vanderbilt,"* the *"Advance Commodore,"* the *"Southwestern Limited,"* the *"Detroiter,"* the *"Wolverine,"* the *"Cleveland Limited,"* the *"Iroquois,"* the *"Ohio State Limited,"* the *"New England States,"* and *"Motor City Special."*

Many of the new ideas making for greater comfort and luxury of these cars are the result of suggestions made in response to questionnaires which were distributed to the New York Central's passengers on its principal trains during the war. Thus, as members of Central's postwar plans committee some 10,000 passengers helped design the equipment of these record making orders.

(Excerpted from Railway Age, December 15, 1945)

NYCSHS Collection

The ex-C&O twin unit diners were used in the *Detroiter* and, on occasion, the *Commodore Vanderbilt.* As trains were discontinued the cars became surplus and since they didn't match any other equipment they were sold to the B&O in early 1957.

D. T. Hayward, Jay Williams Collection

The bedroom side of 10 roomette, 6 double-bedroom *Sagamon River* as it awaits departure from Springfield, Massachusetts on August 31, 1964 on Train 27. The *Sagamon River* was sold to the NdeM in 1966 and renamed *Etiopia.*

Cascade Glory was built by Pullman-Standard in 1938 and sold to NYC in 1948. It was repainted in 1946 and used in secondary train service until 1959 when it was sold to NdeM. Photo taken at Chicago coach yard in 1958.

Burdell Bulgrim, Collection of H. H. Harwood Jr.

NEW YORK CENTRAL'S
NEW Luxury Coaches—
adding enchantment to your first post-war vacation!

FIVE solid gleaming miles of luxury coaches are rolling off the production lines. They're alive with the up-to-the-minute features for which thousands of New York Central passengers voted. And many of these cars of tomorrow are ready today for your first post-war vacation. Ready to carry you, at low coach fares, on your way to the Adirondacks, New England, Niagara Falls, Canada, the Great Lakes or the Western Wonderlands.

Vacation All The Way!
Your vacation starts the minute you board one of these smooth-riding streamlined coaches...with their advanced air conditioning and extra wide sightseeing windows.

Luxury Dressing Rooms!
Smart, spacious dressing lounges feature streamlined fixtures, lighted mirrors, electric outlets for curling iron or razor...the latest appointments for your comfort.

Try This For Size!
Lots of leg room in the new feather-soft reclining seats, instantly adjustable for reading or resting. *And* . . . on many trains, your seat is reserved at no extra charge.

Coming! CARS ENOUGH FOR 52 NEW STREAMLINERS
TO UNDERLINE THE *NEW* IN *NEW* YORK CENTRAL

NEW YORK CENTRAL

The Scenic Water Level Route

Several photos were taken at New York's Mott Haven Yard on October 22, 1959 to be used in advertisements for the new sleepercoach service. This shot shows the side of 10802 and has been assigned car No. SC67, the *Commodore Vanderbilt* section of the *20th Century Limited*.

Budd vs. Pullman, Inc.

When the Budd Company began building sleeping cars in 1936, they quickly ran into opposition from the Pullman Company which had a contract with most of America's passenger carrying railroads to operate their sleeping cars. The Pullman Company refused to staff cars not built by its Pullman-Standard division. This was the foundation of the dispute between Budd and Pullman, Inc., the outcome of which would dramatically change the sleeping car operations in North America.

The Budd Company felt that this was illegal inasmuch as it constituted a monopolistic practice to eliminate competition. They sued Pullman in 1940 for anti-trust violations and in 1944, the court agreed with Budd. The settlement required Pullman, Inc. to divest either the manufacturing division or the Pullman Company. It chose the latter, although the Pullman Company continued to operate cars in the U.S. and Mexico for another twenty years or so.

In 1947-48, the Pullman-owned cars were sold to a consortium of railroads who continued to have Pullman operate them. In 1958, NYC assumed operation of its sleepers, hiring most, if not all, of those Pullman employees who staffed its trains. During regular shopping, the Pullman name slowly disappeared from the cars

Apparently there were a few exceptions. Some of the 1938 *Imperial*-series cars (4-4-2s) were renamed for bridges after being refurbished for use in the *20th Century Limited*. These cars, along with the other *Imperial* cars, were not bought by the NYC in 1948 but remained with the Pullman pool operations. The cars retained the Pullman name in the corners until they were returned to NYC in the mid-1960s by which time the cars seldom saw service and were stored, sold or scrapped.

Have Yourself a **SEE-LEVEL VACATION**

...in air-cooled comfort and all-weather safety...
at New York Central's money-saving round-trip fares!

See exciting New York! Broadway shows and Fifth Avenue shops. Skyscrapers and museums. On the way, see the scenic Hudson from your Central window!

See the Adirondacks! World-famous resorts. Rugged peaks and lovely lakes. New York Central takes you through miles of this mountain wilderness.

See historic New England! Bunker Hill and Plymouth Rock. Seashore and mountains. And, on your way, see the beautiful Berkshires from your cool Dieseliner.

See Niagara Falls and Canada! Niagara's majesty. Old-World Quebec. And, on your way, see the Great Lakes or Mohawk Valley from your train window.

See Western Wonderlands! Deserts, dude ranches, the Rockies, California, the Northwest. Go New York Central's Water Level Route to western gateways!

FREE ILLUSTRATED VACATION GUIDE with fun map of playgrounds. Money-saving tips on baggage and round-trip fares. Send coupon to New York Central, Room 1334HH, 466 Lexington Avenue, New York 17, N. Y.

NAME

ADDRESS

CITY_____STATE

NEW YORK CENTRAL
The Scenic Water Level Route

THE CORRIDORS

For decades, New York Central offered comfortable and convenient travel services between the major cities along its east-west routes. Trains also traveled over NYC's subsidiary lines, Michigan Central Railroad (Chicago-Detroit-Buffalo), Cleveland, Cincinnati, Chicago and St. Louis Railroad ("Big Four") and the Boston and Albany Railroad with connections to other roads such as NYC-controlled Pittsburgh and Lake Erie Railroad. Some of the routes between major cities would eventually become known as "corridors."

Throughout the late 1930s and particularly during the war years, substantial passenger traffic existed between the cities in the Midwest diamond: Chicago-Detroit; Detroit-Cleveland; Cleveland-Cincinnati; and Cincinnati-Chicago. Being competitive, NYC sought to capitalize on this passenger current with the initiation of a new fleet of passenger trains which would be called *Mercury* service.

Not having the capital to invest in new equipment, NYC turned to its mechanical department at Beech Grove shops outside Indianapolis to rebuild a set of Osgood-Bradley-built commuter passenger coaches into a train set consisting of a baggage/coach, coaches, lounge car, dining car, and observation car. In 1936, the train was placed on a schedule between Cleveland and Detroit and was so successful that additional train sets were created for service along the other principal routes.

In 1948, with the new cars from Pullman-Standard, Budd, and ACF about to arrive, the *Mercury* trains and other trains such as the *Midday Michigan*, the *Twilight Limited* and the *Motor City Special*, in addition to the through trains such as the *Niagara*, the *Wolverine* and the *New York Special* were placed on schedules between Chicago and Detroit serving intermediate stops at Woodlawn (63rd Street), Hammond, Gary, Michigan City, Niles, Kalamazoo, Battle Creek, Albion, Grand Rapids, Jackson and Ann Arbor.

Trains between Detroit and Cleveland included Nos. 301, 303 (*Cincinnati Mercury*), 305, 76/761 (*Cleveland Mercury*), 307 (*Indianapolis Express*), 311 and 309 (*Ohio Special*); Nos. 75/750 (*Cleveland Mercury*), 312, 302 (*Michigan Special*), 314, 306, and 310 at Toledo connecting with trains out of Cleveland.

In the Cleveland-Cincinnati corridor, NYC provided service to Wellington, New London, Shelby, Crestline, Galion, Delaware, Columbus, Springfield, Dayton, Middletown, and Winton Place (five miles from Cincinnati). The trains along this route included the *Cincinnati Special*, the *Cleveland-Cincinnati Special*, *Capitol City Special*, *Midnight Special* and the *Ohio State Limited*.

Trains traveling between Cleveland and Cincinnati via Bellefontaine, Ohio included the *Cincinnati Mercury* (starting in 1951), *Michigan Special* and the *Ohio Special*.

Service between Cincinnati and Chicago was provided by the *James Whitcomb Riley* in addition to the *Chicago Special*, *White City Special*, the *Sycamore*, the *Chicago Night Express*; the *New Royal Palm* and the *Ponce de Leon* (through service to Florida via the Southern Railway, Florida East Coast Railway and the Seaboard Air Line Railroad), although the latter two were connecting trains out of Chicago's Central Station which passed coaches and sleeping cars to the Southern at Cincinnati. The same was true of No. 406, the *Carolina Special*, which made important connections to trains of the Chesapeake and Ohio as well as the Southern Railway.

Out of Indianapolis' stately Romanesque Union Station, the sleek limiteds would roll to Chicago through Lafayette and the small farming communities of central

No. 4009 was in the second order of E7s which sported boxy number boards. Coupled with an E7 "B" unit, No. 4009 leads the *Michigan* near Dearborn, Michigan on September 7, 1963. The new Flexivans are slowly replacing mail and express cars. Note the two "standard" coaches ahead of the Budd diner.

Louis A. Marre

Collection of Louis A. Marre

Hudson No. 5391 moves the *Cleveland Special* through Dayton, Ohio on October 23, 1949 with a mix of standard and streamline equipment. The diesels will soon replace the Hudsons, Niagras and Mohawks on the main lines.

Indiana such as Fowler, Earl Park, Sheldon, and northwest to Kankakee before arriving at Central Station on Michigan Avenue.

Another corridor on which frequent service was provided was the St. Louis-Indianapolis route offering through service to Cincinnati and on to Cleveland with stops out of St. Louis at Hillsborough, Pana, Shelbyville (Illinois), Mattoon, Terre Haute and Greencastle, Indiana. Trains traveling onto Cincinnati from Indianapolis normally stopped at Shelbyville (Indiana), Greensburg, Batesville, and Lawrenceburg Junction.

Trains traveling from Indianapolis to Cleveland would normally make stops at Anderson, Muncie, Union City, Sidney, Bellefontaine, Marion, Galion, Crestline, Wellington and then Linndale, six miles short of Cleveland.

Another important route not served by the fleet of *Mercury* trains was the Buffalo-New York corridor. The trains serving this route stopped at Rochester, Syracuse, Rome, Utica, Herkimer, Schenectady, Albany, Poughkeepsie, and at Harmon for a change to electric power.

Among the trains serving this route, aside from the well known through trains, were the *De Witt Clinton*, the *Cayuga*, the *Mohawk*, the *Genesee* and the *Tuscarora*, to name but a few.

The most famous of these trains was the *Empire State Express*, re-equipped with Budd-built passenger cars and the new service inaugurated on December 7, 1941, a publicist's nightmare. While the train actually went beyond Buffalo to serve Cleveland and Detroit, it was principally known as a New York-Buffalo express.

The New York-Buffalo trains provided coach, lounge, and dining services and trains such as the *Upstate Special* even sported Budd-built observation/lounge cars of the Nos. 58-70 series. Other trains which were equipped with these observation cars included the *Twilight Limited*, the *Mercury* trains, the *Sycamore* and *Cincinnati Special*. The coaches in these trains were mostly those from Pullman-Standard, which had provided the most coaches from the 1944 order with stainless stee

NYC passenger trains usually operated with two back-to-back locomotives. On occasion, trains ran with single units. Normally Train No. 355, The *Michigan,* would have two E units but perhaps only the No. 4026 was available on this day in October 1966.

New York—Chatham—Pittsfield—North Adams
(See Harlem Division Time Tables for Local Service, including Parlor and Dining Car Service)

Miles	Table No. 34	5 Note Ex. Sun.	43 Sun. Only	13 Sat. Only	15 Ex. Sat. & Sun.	◆63 Note Fri. Only	59 Sun. Only			
		AM	AM	PM	PM	PM 7 10	PM 7 50			
	Lv New York.......(E. T.) (Grand Central Terminal)	8 47	9 20	1 35	4 32					
4	Lv New York (125th St.)...	b 8 57	h 9 30	h 1 45	h 4 42	h 7 20	h 8 00			
22	Lv White Plains.........	9 22	9 56	h 2 10	h 5 06	h 7 45	h 8 23			
52	Lv Brewster............	10 23	10 45	2 54	5 53	8 36	9 12			
64	Lv Pawling.............	10 46	11 07	3 10	6 15	8 54	9 31			
85	Lv Amenia.............	11 24	11 46	3 42	6 50	9 29	10 06			
93	Lv Millerton...........	11 43	12 03	3 59	7 10	9 45	10 21			
109	Lv Hillsdale...........	12 07	12 28	4 25	7 33	10 10	10 46			
128	Ar Chatham............	12 50	1 08	5 10	8 10	10 57	11 25			

(◆63 column note: Will not run Dec. 26 or Jan. 2, but will run Weds. Dec. 24 and 31.)

Miles		◆620			◆622	◆626		◆612		
0	Lv Chatham............	1 06			5 17	8 15		11 30		
27	Ar Pittsfield..........	1 43			5 54	8 52		12.07		
48	Ar North Adams........	2 27			6 40	9 38		12.53		
		PM			PM	PM		AM		

	38 Sun. Only	◆ 621 Ex. Sun.	76 Sat. Only	◆ 40 Sun. Only	◆ 54 Sun. Only	◆615 Ex. Sat. & Sun.	◆ 629 Sun. Only			
	AM	AM	PM	PM	PM	PM	PM			
Lv North Adams.........		6 05				3 05	6 30			
Lv Pittsfield.........		6 55				3 51	7 16			
Ar Chatham............		7 31				4 30	7 55			

	38	14	76	◆40	◆54	26	◆72			
Lv Chatham............	8 05	8 05	1 35	2 45	6 00	6 15	8 00			
Lv Hillsdale..........	8 34	8 38	2 08	3 17	6 29	6 48	8 28			
Lv Millerton..........	9 02	9 08	2 36	3 48	7 00	7 15	8 54			
Lv Amenia.............	9 14	9 19	2 51	4 01	7 12	7 29				
Lv Pawling............	9 45	9 54	3 28	4 40	7 45	8 12	9 31			
Lv Brewster...........	10 03	10 18	3 45	5 05	8 05	8 36				
Ar White Plains.......	10 46	11 02	5 12	5 54	8 51	9 48	10 31			
Ar New York (125th St.)..	¡11 09	11 27	¿ 6 17	6 17	¿ 9 14	10 15	¡10 55			
Ar New York (Grand Central Terminal)..	11 20	11 40	6 51	6 30	9 25	10 31	11 06			
	AM	AM	PM	PM	PM	PM	PM			

Westfield—Chautauqua—Jamestown
(Via Central Greyhound Lines, Inc., of New York)

Table No. 35	Ex. Sun. & Hol.	Daily	Daily	Ex. Sun. & Hol.	Sun. only
	AM	AM	PM	PM	PM
Lv Westfield.(E. T.)	8 00	10 00	12 05	3 55	6 10
Ar Chautauqua....	8 35	10 35	12 40	4 30	6 40
Ar Jamestown.....	9 10	11 10	1 15	5 05	7 15
	AM	AM	PM	PM	PM

	Ex. Sun. & Hol.	Daily	Daily	Daily
	AM	AM	PM	PM
Lv Jamestown(E.T.)	8 00	9 45	1 00	4 20
Lv Chautauqua....	8 35	10 20	1 35	4 55
Ar Westfield......	9 05	10 45	2 05	5 25
	AM	AM	PM	PM

Albany—North Adams
(Beeliner Service)

◆620 Ex. Sun.	Table No. 36	◆621 Ex. Sun.	◆615 Ex. Sat. & Sun.
PM		AM	PM
12 35	Lv Albany..... Ar	8 12	5 12
1 05	Ar Chatham... Ar	7 31	4 30
1 43	Ar Pittsfield.. Ar	6 54	3 50
2 15	Ar Adams..... Ar	6 18	3 18
2 27	Ar No. Adams Lv	6 05	3 05
PM		AM	PM

For explanation of Reference Marks. See Page 5.   For Pullman, Coach and Dining Car Service. see Pages 6 to 13.

The corridors were not restricted to the Midwest as is witnessed by this December 1952 timetable.

fluting. The cars were actually made of Cor-Ten steel with the fluting panels hung on clips, not unlike aluminum siding. This type of construction would later result in serious rusting problems for the carriers which bought this type of car.

With the advent of the interstate highway system in the 1950s, the passenger service in the Midwest diamond evaporated and patrons found it more convenient to drive to their destinations. With airplane travel becoming more sophisticated, what traffic was left couldn't justify the continuation of many of the trains and invariably services were cut back or eliminated.

As the turn of another century is in sight, the pendulum of circumstance has swung back to the reappraisal of rail passenger traffic in the corridors once served by the trains of the New York Central. While it is doubtful that the level of service would even approach that of the great passenger fleet that once served the many cities of Michigan, Indiana, and Ohio, it is important to have a standard by which any new and revitalized service can be judged.

Collection of Louis A. Marre

The *Twilight Limited* departs Detroit on May 29, 1961 with coaches, 6-double bedroom lounge (as parlor), diner and observation car. No. 4048, an E8 with an E7 trailing, is equipped with a multiple unit connection on the nose. Quite often the small door would fly open when the speed of the train rose over 50 MPH.

"Subsidy"

Mohawk Airlines is one of 13 local air operators in the U. S. which receive a direct Federal break-even subsidy out of regard for the expensive, short-haul nature of their service. Its expenses outpace revenues by 42.8 per cent; a subsidy makes up the difference. Mohawk operates, among other services, nonstop Convair 240 flights between New York and Syracuse. Running time is 1 hour 8 minutes, fare is $14.95. Now, New York-Syracuse is 289-1/2 miles by New York Central and is considered profitable passenger territory. The Empire State Express make the run west in 5 hours 35 minutes, charges $11.33 in coaches, $19.60 first class plus parlor-car seat. Because of the fare differential made possible by subsidy, more and more travelers are shifting from the depot to the airport. But would they, asks a railroad spokesman, if Mohawk boosted fares 42.8 per cent to eliminate the direct subsidy and charged $21.35 as a result? P.S.: this illustration makes no allowance for indirect airport and airway subsidies. Another P.S.: In 1955 American and Mohawk airlines handled 352 passengers a day at Syracuse vs. 440 in 1957. New York Central handled 341 a day in 1955, only 244 in 1957.

Of all modes of transport in the U.S., the railroad (and hence the passenger train) is the only one excluding pipelines which provides and maintains its own physical plant out of private capital and is taxed as a property owner.

from "Who Shot the Passenger Train?"
by David P. Morgan
TRAINS, April 1959

H. H. Harwood Jr.

A re-engined Baldwin "Babyface" locomotive or "Gravel Gertie" (as they were known on the NYC), leads a passenger F3 "B" unit on the *Sycamore* out of Cincinnati in April 1956. Cincinnati Union Terminal looks pretty quiet, but weeds haven't had a chance to grow… yet.

Collection of H. H. Harwood Jr.

he *Cincinnati Special*, Train 416 (Chicago-Cincinnati), heads for its namesake city with a mix of equipment led by two Hudsons the summer of 1955. Even at this time NYC was integrating the old standard cars with the newer ones on the secondary ns. The train even carries a generic tail sign.

J. A. Pinkepank, Collection of Louis A. Marre

A glimpse of the future in August 1960. NYC GP9 and 5934 is the yard switcher positioning the Pennsylvania's *Northern Arrow*, a Cincinnati-Mackinaw City, all-Pullman and weekend-only limited. Regular power for the train was two Pennsylvania E8s. The GP9 was based at Mackinaw City for switching duty.

J. W. Swanberg

Not all trains in the Great Steel Fleet were drawn by sleek passenger units. Here is the *Hendrick Hudson*, Train 54, a Buffalo to Grand Central workhorse. It is led by Alco RS-3s No. 8291 and 8292 at Roa Hook, north of Peekskill, New York on September 8, 1962. Train 54 carried a parlor-buffet lounge in addition to coaches.

Peoria & Eastern Ry.
(Operated by N. Y. C. R. R. Co.)
Peoria—Bloomington—Indianapolis

Miles	Table No. 19	12 Daily		11 Daily
		PM		AM
0.0	Lv Peoria (Union Station)..(C.T.)	2 05	Lv Indianapolis (UnionSta.) (C.T.)	7 00
9.0	Lv Pekin	2 35	Lv Crawfordsville	7 56
18.0	Lv Tremont	2 49	Lv Waynetown	8 08
25.2	Lv Mackinaw	3 00	Lv Hillsborough	8 15
34.9	Lv Danvers	3 12	Lv Veedersburg	8 24
44.7	Lv Bloomington	3 33	Lv Covington	8 35
54.4	Lv Downs	3 48	Lv Danville (Ill.)	9 08
60.9	Lv Le Roy	3 55	Lv Oakwood	9 20
70.0	Lv Farmer City	4 05	Lv Muncie	f 9 24
73.0	Lv Harris	f 4 09	Lv Fithian	9 27
77.7	Lv Mansfield	4 15	Lv Ogden	9 34
83.4	Lv Mahomet	4 22	Lv St. Joseph	9 41
93.2	Lv Champaign	4 45	Lv Mayview	f 9 45
95.3	Lv Urbana	4 51	Lv Urbana	10 06
100.6	Lv Mayview	f 5 04	Lv Champaign	10 30
103.6	Lv St. Joseph	f 5 09	Lv Mahomet	10 40
108.8	Lv Ogden	f 5 14	Lv Mansfield	10 46
113.3	Lv Fithian	f 5 19	Lv Harris	f10 51
114.5	Lv Muncie	f 5 21	Lv Farmer City	10 56
118.3	Lv Oakwood	f 5 26	Lv Le Roy	11 08
126.4	Lv Danville (Ill.)	5 50	Lv Downs	f11 16
139.2	Lv Covington	6 08	Lv Bloomington	11 50
146.7	Lv Veedersburg	6 20	Lv Danvers	12 02
152.1	Lv Hillsborough	f 6 27	Lv Mackinaw	12 14
157.4	Lv Waynetown	f 6 32	Lv Tremont	12 25
167.6	Lv Crawfordsville	6 50	Lv Pekin	12 45
211.4	Ar Indianapolis (Union Station)	7 45	Ar Peoria (Union Station)	1 10
		PM		PM

(Both center columns labeled: THE PEORIAN)

CHICAGO · DETROIT · CLEVELAND · INDIANAPOLIS · COLUMBUS · CINCINNATI

TRAVEL CAREFREE
BY DAY THROUGH THE
"HEART of the MID-WEST"

CHICAGO MERCURY
Parlor observation—streamlined diner — coach tavern lounge—reserved seat coaches. Mornings east and west, CHICAGO—DETROIT.

TWILIGHT LIMITED
Late afternoon twin of the morning **Mercury.**

CLEVELAND MERCURY
Parlor observation car, reserved-seat coaches, tavern lounge, diner. CLEVELAND to DETROIT morning; return afternoons.

CINCINNATI MERCURY
Parlor observation car, coaches with center smoking lounges, diner. Mornings, CLEVELAND to CINCINNATI; return afternoons.

JAMES WHITCOMB RILEY
All-reserved-seat coach streamliner. Coach observation car. Famous dining service. Mornings, CINCINNATI-CHICAGO; return afternoons.

W. D. Edson

The NYC subsidiary Peoria and Eastern carded two trains between Peoria and Indianapolis. Power consisted of a GP7 equipped with a steam generator and silver trucks. Here Train 11 stops to pick up and unload express at Danville, Illinois on September 28, 1953.

Observation car "Chicago" brings up the rear of the *Mercury* as it leaves Cincinnati Union Terminal behind. NYC trains either originated or terminated in Cincinnati - they did not operate through to other cities. Niagara No. 6021 seems to move the train out with ease and a clear stack.

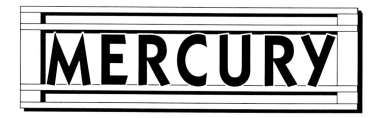

THE MERCURY TRAINS

Nos. 375 and 376
Nos. 761-76 and 424, 401-402

The *Mercury* trains of 1948 carried on a tradition from the prewar era. The trains included the original equipment which survived into the mid-1950s before the new coaches, diners and lounge cars completely replaced the cars which had been rebuilt in the 1930s at Beech Grove shops (from coaches which had been built in the 1920s!).

Immensely popular in the pre-war years, *Mercury* service was provided between Chicago and Detroit, Detroit-Cleveland and Cleveland-Cincinnati. The *James Whitcomb Riley* was a *"Mercury"* by another name serving the Chicago-Cincinnati corridor.

The trains carried parlor cars, a lounge car, dining car (with its own distinctive dining china), coaches and observation cars. In 1956, however, as the cuts in service were made, No. 375, the *Chicago Mercury*, lost its observation car between Detroit and Chicago and the *Cleveland Mercury* picked up a 10-6 from No. 57, the *Cleveland Limited*, at Cleveland for Toledo.

In 1956, the *Mercury* trains' schedules were altered slightly with the anticipated arrival of the *Aerotrain* and *Xplorer*, that NYC advertised as "The Trains of the Future." The new trains would ostensibly take over the routes and lure back to the rails the passenger traffic being lost to the highways and to the airlines. That was the plan.

Unfortunately, beset with mechanical difficulties and rough riding characteristics, the new trains never fulfilled their intended role, only creating further erosion of a deteriorating and dwindling passenger base in the Detroit-Cleveland, Cleveland-Cincinnati market.

In October 1957, the *Cleveland-Cincinnati Mercury* was dropped and by April 1958 only the *Cleveland Mercury* (Detroit-Cleveland), now Nos. 75-76 westbound and 77-78 eastbound, remained. The *Chicago Mercury* had also disappeared with service supplanted by the *Wolverine*. By 1959 even the *Cleveland Mercury* was gone, another victim of the superhighway and "friendly skies."

Collection of Louis A. Marre

he *Xplorer* at Beech Grove, Indiana on June 1, 1956. Designed to be lightweight and high speed, the train fulfilled the former ut mechanical problems handicapped the later. It was intended to be a train of the future, but it fell short of its billing and as removed from service a little over a year later.

Cincinnati to Dayton, Columbus and Cleveland

Table No. 23

Miles	Station	444	402	312	◆422	424	16	442	302
		Daily	Daily Note	Daily	Daily Note	Daily	Daily	Daily	Daily
		CAPITAL CITY SPECIAL	THE CINCINNATI MERCURY—Will operate until Sept. 29, incl., unless sooner changed or extended	THE QUEEN CITY	OHIO Xplorer Will operate until Sept. 29, incl. unless sooner changed or extended	CLEVELAND SPECIAL	OHIO STATE LIMITED Through Train To New York	NIGHT SPECIAL	MICHIGAN SPECIAL
		AM	AM	AM	PM	PM	PM	PM	PM
0.0	Lv **Cincinnati** (E.T.) (Union Terminal)		8 45	9 00	1 45	3 30	4 20	11 00	11 30
4.7	Lv Winton Place		8 56	9 11	L 1 56	3 41	4 31	11 11	11 41
31.5	Lv **Middletown**		9 32	9 45	2 29	4 14	5 01	11 49	12 17
42.3	Lv Miamisburg		......	......	......	......	......	......	......
52.3	Lv **Dayton**		10 05	10 15	2 57	4 42	5 26	12 28	12 50
63.6	Lv Fairborn		......	......	......	......	......	......	......
77.4	Ar **Springfield**		10 45	11 00	3 35	5 20	6 05	1 13	1 35
77.4	Lv **Springfield**		10 45	......	3 35	5 20	6 05	1 13	......
96.9	Lv London		♠11 09	......	......	......	......	......	......
122.4	Ar **Columbus**	......	11 38	......	4 22	6 07	6 57	2 05	
122.4	Lv **Columbus**	8 10	11 50	......	4 30	6 20	7 07	2 35	
146.5	Lv Delaware	8 46	12 26		......	......	......	......	
163.1	Lv Cardington	♠9 03	......		......	......	......	......	
167.7	Lv Edison (Mt. Gilead)	♠9 08	†12 48		......	......	......	......	
180.6	Lv Galion	9 30	1 15		5 31	7 21	g8 07	3 55	
184.8	Lv Crestline	9 40	1 31		5 40	7 30		4 17	
193.3	Lv Shelby	9 52	1 50		b 5 51	b 7 41			......
205.5	Lv Greenwich	......	......		......	......			......
213.0	Lv New London	10 13	♠2 13		......	......			......
224.0	Lv Wellington	10 31	2 30		G 6 20	♠8 10			......
235.1	Lv Grafton	♠10 45	......		......	......			......
253.8	Lv Linndale	11 05	3 05	......	G 7 00	8 45		5 30	......
260.0	Ar **Cleveland** (Union Terminal)	11 20	3 20	......	7 15	9 00		5 45	......
		AM	PM	AM	PM	PM	PM	AM	AM

Cleveland to Columbus, Dayton and Cincinnati

Station	309	15	◆421	303	433	401	445	417
	Daily	Daily	Daily Note	Daily	Daily	Daily Note	Daily	Daily
	OHIO SPECIAL	OHIO STATE LIMITED	OHIO Xplorer Will operate until Sept. 29, incl. unless sooner changed or extended	THE QUEEN CITY	CLEVELAND CINCINNATI SPECIAL	THE CINCINNATI MERCURY – Will operate until Sept. 29, incl., unless sooner changed or extended	CAPITAL CITY SPECIAL	MIDNIGHT SPECIAL
	AM	AM	AM	PM	PM	PM	PM	PM
Lv **Cleveland** (E.T.) (Union Ter.)	......	......	6 45	......	12 05	5 00	7 00	11 4
Lv Linndale	......		L6 55	......	12 15	L 5 10	7 10	11 5
Lv Grafton	......		......	......	......	......	7 39	......
Lv Wellington	......		L7 30	......	12 52	L 5 47	7 52	......
Lv New London	......		......	......	......	......	ss 8 06	......
Lv Greenwich	......		......	......	......	......	......	......
Lv Shelby			7 58		1 25	6 18	8 28	# 1 0
Lv Crestline		......	......		1 40	......	8 44	1 2
Lv Galion		4 07	8 15		1 55	6 35	9 01	1 4
Lv Edison (Mt. Gilead)		......	......		......	......	9 21	......
Lv Cardington		......	......		......	......	......	......
Lv Delaware		......	......		2 35	......	9 48	......
Ar **Columbus**		5 11	9 17		3 12	7 38	10 25	2 5
Lv **Columbus**	......	5 21	9 23	......	3 30	7 48		3
Lv London	......	......	......	......	......	......		......
Ar **Springfield**	......	6 20	10 18	......	4 35	8 43		4
Lv **Springfield**	4 32	6 20	10 18	4 05	4 35	8 43		4
Lv Fairborn	......	......	......	......	......	......		......
Lv **Dayton**	5 20	7 01	10 59	4 46	5 16	9 24		5
Lv Miamisburg	A 5 33	......	......	......	......	......		......
Lv **Middletown**	5 55	7 25	11 25	5 12	5 43	9 50		6
Lv Winton Place	6 36	8 04	G12 05	5 53	6 24	G10 29		6
Ar **Cincinnati** (Union Ter.)	6 45	8 15	12 15	6 05	6 35	10 40		7
	AM	AM	PM	PM	PM	PM	PM	AM

Cincinnati—Dayton—Toledo—Detroit

Table No. 24

Miles	Station	312	302
		Daily	Daily
		THE QUEEN CITY	MICHIGAN SPECIAL
		AM	PM
0.0	Lv **Cincinnati** (E.T.) (Union Terminal)	9 00	11 30
4.7	Lv Winton Place	9 11	11 41
31.5	Lv **Middletown**	9 45	12 17
42.3	Lv Miamisburg	......	......
52.3	Lv **Dayton**	10 15	12 50
77.4	Ar **Springfield**	11 00	1 35
77.4	Lv **Springfield**	11 00	1 35
92.1	Lv Urbana	11 17	1 53
110.0	Ar **Bellefontaine**	11 40	2 19
110.0	Lv **Bellefontaine**	11 49	2 29
134.1	Lv Kenton	12 23	xx3 00
146.1	Lv Forest	......	......
158.5	Lv Carey	12 55	3 30
177.2	Lv Fostoria	1 25	♠ 4 00
212.7	Ar **Toledo**	2 25	4 58
212.7	Lv **Toledo**	2 45	5 20
236.3	Lv Monroe	3 17	5 55
260.0	Lv Wyandotte	3 43	6 25
270.3	Ar **Detroit**	4 05	6 50
		PM	AM

Station	303	309
	Daily	Daily
	THE QUEEN CITY	OHIO SPECIAL
	AM	PM
Lv **Detroit** (E.T.)	11 00	11 35
Lv Wyandotte	11 20	11.56
Lv Monroe	11 47	12 25
Ar **Toledo**	12 25	1 05
Lv **Toledo**	12 35	1 20
Lv Fostoria	1 24	♠ 2 11
Lv Carey	1 55	2 35
Lv Forest	......	......
Lv Kenton	2 26	♠ 3 03
Ar **Bellefontaine**	2 56	3 33
Lv **Bellefontaine**	3 08	3 43
Lv Urbana	3 31	4 05
Ar **Springfield**	4 05	4 32
Lv **Springfield**	4 05	4 32
Lv **Dayton**	4 46	5 20
Lv Miamisburg	......	A5 33
Lv **Middletown**	5 12	5 55
Lv Winton Place	5 53	6 36
Ar **Cincinnati** (Union Terminal)	6 05	6 45
	PM	AM

Now You Can Ride THE OHIO Xplorer

Between Cleveland . . . Columbus

Springfield . . . Dayton

. . . Cincinnati

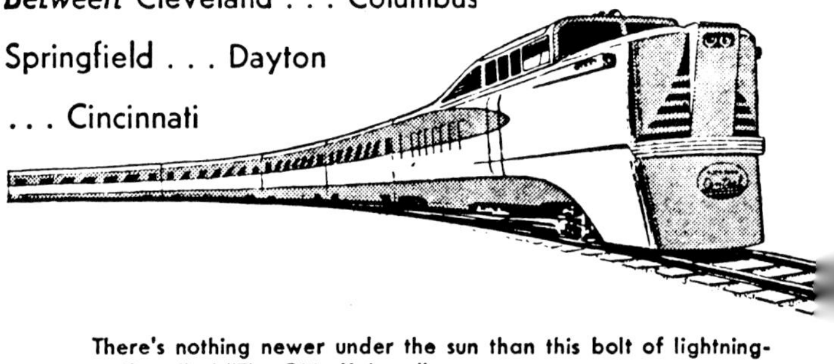

There's nothing newer under the sun than this bolt of lightning-on-rails called "The Ohio Xplorer".

It's lithe and lean, with a gleaming blue and yellow, all aluminum body. It's low and road hugging—two-and-a-half-feet lower than conventional trains.

You ride on springs of soft air. Torsion units level out your ride.

Food service on the "Cruisin' Susan" comes right to your seat. For schedules see Table No. 23 above.

Service between Cleveland, Cincinnati and Detroit was provided by a variety of trains in the summer of 1956, including the ill-fated *Xplorer.*

NEW YORK CENTRAL SYSTEM

Robert A. Hadley, Jay Williams Collection

One of the two Hudson type locomotives especially streamlined for the *Empire State Express* has been assigned to the *Mercury*, een here pulling a mix of the new and old coach cars. The locomotive has two cast plates on its front—a NYC oval and just bove that a plate reading "The Mercury."

The *Xplorer* passes through Goshen, Indiana on April 18, 1956 in a scene which would become more common. The *Xplorer's* engine, No. 20 was not yet ready so the train is being test run with E8 No. 4073. The *Xplorer* was championed by Robert R. Young while he was at the C&O, but he took over NYC before it was built, so he brought it to NYC rails. By 1956, passenger train service (and NYC) was in serious trouble and needed a miracle. Despite the high hopes, this was not it.

Herbert Hamish
Arthur Shull, Jr. Collection

H. H. Harwood

Mohawk No. 3110 is resting after its run from Cleveland with the Cincinnati *Mercury* in August 1953. This is quite a contra with the Xplorer above.

The *Mercury* departs Cincinnati on June 27, 1954 with one of the largest locomotives on NYC's steam roster, No. 6021. The Niagras had a short lifespan of ten years. Built in 1945-46 for main line service, they were moved west in 1952 and finished off their careers on the lines of the Big Four.

Collection of Louis A. Marre

A typical NYC diner setting aboard the *Mercury* shows a variety of marked china, glassware and flatware.

The *Twilight Limited* awaits its passengers in La Salle Street Station in March 1950.

THE TWILIGHT LIMITED

Nos. 30 and 31
Nos. 356 and 357

The Chicago-Detroit "corridor" was always an important run and New York Central fielded several trains (the *Chicago Mercury*, *Motor City Special*, *New York Special* and the *Wolverine*) to provide frequent, convenient service. One of the longest lasting trains was the *Twilight Limited*, Nos. 30 and 31, scheduled for a late afternoon departure from both Chicago (Central Station until 1957) and Detroit for the five-hour run over the Michigan Central route. Both Nos. 30 and 31 (until 1958) were equipped with Budd-built observation cars of the 58-71-series, parlor service (often a sleeper-as-parlor car —a 6-double bedroom/lounge or a 22-roomette) tavern/lounge, diner, and coaches.

For most of the next 20 years after 1948, the *Twilight Limited* kept to its roughly 5:00 P.M. departure schedule from both cities with stops at Gary, Niles, Kalamazoo, Battle Creek, Jackson, and Ann Arbor. With the April 1957 timetable change, the *Twilight Limited* departed from La Salle Street Station leaving the Chicago-Cincinnati "Big Four" trains at Illinois Central Railroad's Central Station.

In 1958, the parlor cars were replaced with a "sleeper-as-parlor" Detroit-Chicago although in 1959 the eastbound parlor was back. With the April 1958 timetable Nos. 30 and 31 became Nos. 356 and 357.

Reference to the parlor cars disappeared again in October 1961 (the observation "parlor" still remained—until April 1964) when the sleeper-as-parlor returned, until 1965. Dining and lounge service was also retained and in 1965 the train acquired one of the ex-*Stream/Lake* 6-bedroom/lounge cars, renumbered, and billed as a "parlor buffet-lounge."

In April 1966, bereft of its observation, the *Twilight Limited* offered a diner-lounge, sleeper-as-parlor and coaches. By October 1966, as more service cuts were instituted, the trains carried a diner/lounge (one of the 450-467-series) and coaches and in April 1967 briefly became coach-only. In November 1967, however, the diner was back until the Penn Central merger.

E.L. Thompson, H.H. Harwood Jr. Collection

Detroit's Michigan Central Terminal is seen in this view looking west from 15th Street on July 15, 1950, where the *Twilight Limited* is about to depart at 4:45. It will arrive in Chicago's Central Station five hours later. Today this massive structure has been abandoned to the vandals and has become a gutted ruin.

Louis A. Marr

NYC's first E7, No. 4000 leads the *Twilight Limited* into the sunset with an RPO, baggage coach and a mix of Pullman-Standard and Budd equipment at Dearborn, Michigan on September 5, 1965.

No. 30—EASTBOUND
No. 31—WESTBOUND
THE TWILIGHT LIMITED—DAILY
ALL SEATS IN PARLOR CARS AND COACHES
ARE RESERVED

Observation Parlor Car (N. Y. C. Car)
    Chicago and Detroit
Parlor Car—Sleeper as Parlor Car
    Detroit to Chicago (Ex. Sat.) (Westbound Only)
Dining Service
Lounge Car (Beverages)
    Chicago and Detroit
Reclining Seat Coaches—Porter Service
    Chicago and Detroit

No longer a "streamliner" but still a premier train in October 1957.

THE
TWILIGHT
LIMITED

NEW YORK CENTRAL SYSTEM

As fewer passengers were carried, express freight traffic became more important to defray costs. Here the eastbound *Twilight Limited* crosses the St. Joseph River near Niles, Michigan on July 9, 1965. This evening No. 356 carries one Flexivan car. The cigar band paint scheme is pretty drab compared to the lightning stripes.

Both: Louis A. Marre

Observation-lounge No. 61 graces the rear of the *Twilight Limited* at Dearborn, Michigan on September 8, 1963. The diner just ahead is of the 691-699 or 447-449 series. A vestibule door on one side of the car, forward in the picture, differentiated the car on the exterior from the grill diner, along with the placement of the smaller kitchen windows. The tavern lounge car, 35-47 series, is just ahead of the diner. The coaches are Pullman-Standard

Collection of Bob's Photo

The *James Whitcomb Riley* near Lafayette, Indiana in October 1947. The observation car appears to be standing room only
This car, like the others built for *Mercury* service, was originally a commuter coach rebuilt by NYC at Beech Grove Shops. It
would be retired with the arrival of the new Budd built observations Nos. 48-52.

JAMES WHITCOMB RILEY
Nos. 3 and 4

The *James Whitcomb Riley*, named for Indiana's famous literary figure or *"Riley,"* as it was known, operated over the Cleveland, Cincinnati, Chicago, & St. Louis Railroad subsidiary and was the star of the "Big Four" routes Chicago-Indianapolis-Cincinnati corridor. Other trains in this important service included the *Booth Tarkington,* the *Sycamore,* and the *Midwestern.*

While Nos. 3 and 4 carried a mix of Pullman-Standard and Budd-built coaches and offered dining service in one or often two back-to-back diners, the train did not offer parlor service like its Chicago-Detroit counterpart, although it did carry an observation lounge (of the 48-51 series) and in the 1950s carried a through-sleeper from the Southern Railway at Cincinnati. No. 3 was carded for an early 8:30 A.M. departure from the Queen City with stops at Indianapolis, Lafayette, Kankakee, and Woodlawn with a 12:55 P.M. arrival at Chicago; Central Station. The westbound Riley left Chicago for Cincinnati at 4:40 P.M. with arrival at 11:10 P.M.

In 1953, No. 3 carried a Pullman operated 14-roomette/4-double bedroom sleeper from Southern Railway train No. 28 originating in Asheville, North Carolina. Connecting service was made at Cincinnati.

In 1955, No. 3's schedule was lengthened to include stops at Greensburg and Shelbyville, Indiana with a 1:10 P.M. arrival in Chicago. The dining services were listed as a "thrift grill" but in 1956, the "thrift" disappeared and "dining service" resumed. Also, the Southern Railway substituted a 10-6 for the 14-4 and in October 1956, the *Riley* picked up another 10-6, this one from Newport News, Virginia from C&O train No.1-41 at Cincinnati. This necessitated only a minor lengthening of the train's schedule, leaving Cincinnati at 8:15 A.M. with arrival at Chicago Central Station at 1:15 P.M. Eastbound, No. 4 left Chicago at 4:20 P.M. for an 11:00 P.M. arrival at Cincinnati Union Terminal.

In the April 1958 restructuring, Nos. 3 and 4 became Nos. 303 and 304 with no change in its equipment other than No. 304 carried an eastbound 10-6 for Charlottesville, Virginia, via the C&O from Cincinnati for the summer.

In April 1959, No. 303 carried a Richmond-Chicago 10-6 and a Clifton Forge, Virginia-Chicago 10-6, and on No. 304, through-sleeper service from Chicago to Charlottesville (a 10-6) and Clifton Forge (a 10-6) via the C&O through Cincinnati. With the schedule change, the *Riley* also lost its observation cars.

THE *James Whitcomb Riley*

NEW DE-LUXE ALL COACH STREAMLINER
CINCINNATI • INDIANAPOLIS • LAFAYETTE • CHICAGO

NEW YORK CENTRAL SYSTEM

Brochure issued to commemorate the "new" *James Whitcomb Riley* in 1941.

By 1960, the *Riley* still left from Illinois Central's lake front station, but at 4:30 P.M. for a 10:25 P.M. arrival at CUT with stops at Woodlawn, Kankakee, Lafayette, Indianapolis, Shelbyville, Greensburg and Batesville. No. 303's 8:30 A.M. departure remained.

The *Riley* would be about the only train to last to the end without a major reduction in service or equipment. With the December 1967 consolidation of trains, the *Riley*, still departing from Central Station, was the only NYC train to retain its name and sported through-sleepers off the C&O with only slightly longer schedules (by about 10 minutes). The *Riley* would last into the Penn Central era and Amtrak, albeit the latter operated over a different route.

Re-Equipped "Riley" in Service

A completely re-equipped "James Whitcomb Riley" made its initial run on the New York Central between Cincinnati, Ohio, Indianapolis, Indiana, and Chicago on April 14. The all-coach train consists of 11 cars of the latest design, including two dining cars built by the Budd Company, 7 coaches *(built by the Pullman-Standard Car Manufacturing Company)*, an observation-lounge car *(also built by the Budd Company)*, and a combination baggage car and coach *(built by the American Car & Foundry Company)*.

The new dining cars each seat 44 passengers, and the coaches accommodate 64. The new observation car consists of three sections - a club section at the forward end seating 22 persons, a lounge section in the middle accommodating 21 passengers and an observation section at the rear for an additional 10 passengers.

Note: italics are included from subsequent "correction" of the article which incorrectly identified the observation car and combination baggage car as being built by Pullman-Standard.

(Excerpted from Railway Age - April 24, 1948)

CHICAGO—ASHEVILLE—GREENSBORO—COLUMBIA
(Via Cincinnati and Southern Railway)

Table No. 8

READ DOWN

302 Daily		
8 55 AM	Lv *Chicago* .... (CST) Ar	
9 55	Lv **CHICAGO** (Cent. Sta.) .... (CDT) Ar	
h11 00	Kankakee	
12 29	Lafayette .... (CDT)	
2 15	Indianapolis .... (EST)	
4 50	Ar **CINCINNATI** (Union Term.) .... (EST) Lv	

READ UP (303 Daily)

303 Daily
1 30 PM
2 30
1 21
11 50
10 30
8 30

All Coach Seats Reserved

Southern Railway (1-2b / 27-2)

9 30	Lv **CINCINNATI** .... (EST) Ar	7 15
6 50	Ar Knoxville Lv	9 40
11 00	Asheville	5 30
5 10	Winston-Salem	8 30
6 05	Greensboro	7 05
11 57	Hendersonville	4 10
12 54	Tryon	3 08
1 55	Spartanburg	2 15
4 45	Ar **COLUMBIA** .... (EST) Lv	11 20
PM		AM

CINCINNATI—INDIANAPOLIS—CHICAGO

Table No. 9

READ DOWN — THE JAMES WHITCOMB RILEY / All Coach Seats Reserved / See Pages 18-19 / THE SYCAMORE

303 Daily Note	305 Daily	Miles		302 Daily	304 Daily Note
AM	PM	0 0	Lv **CINCINNATI** (Union Term.)....(EST) Ar	PM	PM
8 30	4 00			4 50	10 55
9 16	4 46	47 1	Batesville(NCB)	3 40	9 48
9 31	5 01	62 1	Greensburg	3 20	9 34
9 52	5 22	82 1	Shelbyville	2 52	9 11
10 30	6 00	108 9	**INDIANAPOLIS**(EST) Lv	2 10	8 40
10 40	6 15	108 9	**INDIANAPOLIS**(EST) Ar	1 55	8 30
		137 6	Lebanon(NCB)....(CDT)	1 15	
11 50	7 25	173 3	Lafayette	12 25	7 12
		201 5	Fowler(NCB)	11 42	
1 21	9 00	248 1	Kankakee	h11 00	6 00
2 15	9 50	296 0	Woodlawn(NCB)	L1005	E 5 10
2 30	10 05	302 5	Ar **CHICAGO**.....(CDT) Lv	9 55	5 00
PM	PM		(Cent. Sta.)	AM	PM
1 30	9 05		Ar *Chicago* .... (CST) Lv	8 55	4 00

READ UP — THE JAMES WHITCOMB RILEY / All Coach Seats Reserved / See Pages 18-19 / CINCINNATI SPECIAL

CINCINNATI—CLEVELAND—HAMILTON—TORONTO

Table No. 12

READ DOWN

16 Daily	222 Daily		READ UP 327 Daily	329 Daily
PM	AM		AM	PM
2 45	......	Lv **CINCINNATI** (EST) Ar	6 45	1 30
3 57	......	DAYTON	5 15	12 10
5 35	......	COLUMBUS	1 55	10 25
9 15	......	Ar **CLEVELAND** (EDT) Lv	11 45	8 45

28 Daily	222 Daily		51 Daily	57 Ex.Sun
11 08	11 50	Lv **CLEVELAND** (EDT) Ar	9 00	8 00
12 45	2 00	ERIE	6 53	6 05
2 15	4 10	Ar **BUFFALO** .. (EDT) Lv	5 10	4 44

371-322 Daily	379-328 Daily		321-372 Daily	329-376 Daily
5 20	6 00	Lv **BUFFALO** ...(EDT) Ar	12 45	12 15
7 25	8 30	Ar **HAMILTON**	10 20	10 10
8 40	9 45	Ar **TORONTO** ...(EDT) Lv	9 05	8 50
AM	PM	(C.P.Py.) (Union Sta.)	AM	PM

EXPLANATION OF REFERENCE MARKS

CDT—Central Daylight Time
CST—Central Standard Time
EDT—Eastern Daylight Time
EST—Eastern Standard Time
† Daily except Sunday.
f Stops on signal to receive or discharge passengers.
h Stops only to receive passengers.
i Stops only to discharge passengers.
A On Saturdays leave Toronto 11:15 P.M., arrive Smith Falls 5:50 A.M., Montreal 8:45 A.M.
C On Saturday nights leave Chicago 10:59 P.M. Standard Time — 11:59 P.M. Daylight Time.
E Stops to receive passengers for Lafayette and beyond.
L Stops on signal to receive passengers.
S All seats reserved and assigned in advance.
NCB No facilities for handling baggage at this station. Baggage should be checked to or from nearest station where facilities are available.

By 1963, service between Cincinnati and Chicago was limited.

Photo by: Bob Lorenz, Jay Williams Collection

ohawk No. 3144 pulls the *James Whitcomb Riley* near Acton, Indiana, east of Indianapolis in 1954. The Mohawk is adorned ith "elephant ears", which drove the smoke up and over the train at high speed. The second car is a Southern Pullman-andard 10-6 from Asheville, North Carolina.

J. David Ingles, Collection of Louis A. Marre

The *James Whitcomb Riley* approaches Homewood, Illinois on July 12, 1965 with two GP9s and a GP7 leading a train which includes a C&O 10-6 behind the head end cars. Business appears to be good. The "Riley" is on Illinois Central tracks heading for Central Station.

Through the early 1950s The *James Whitcomb Riley* was led by steam power and is seen here as it heads west to Indianapolis and Chicago in July 1951. With the exception of the observation lounge, diner and baggage coach the coaches were the domain of Pullman-Standard. The sleepers off the Southern and C&O ran up front.

H.H. Harwood Jr. Collection

No. 3—THE JAMES WHITCOMB RILEY—DAILY WESTBOUND

ALL COACH SEATS RESERVED—PORTER SERVICE

Sleeping Cars
Asheville, N. C. to Chicago (10 Roomette-6 Double Bedroom)—*From Sou. Ry. No. 28 at Cincinnati*
Newport News, Va. to Chicago (10 Roomette-6 Double Bedroom)—*From C. & O. 41-1 at Cincinnati*

Dining Service

Observation Lounge Car (Beverages),
Cincinnati to Chicago

Reclining Seat Coaches!
Cincinnati to Chicago

No. 4—THE JAMES WHITCOMB RILEY—Daily EASTBOUND

ALL COACH SEATS RESERVED—PORTER SERVICE

Sleeping Car
Chicago to Newport News, Va. (10 Roomette-6 Double Bedroom)—*In C. & O. No. 4-46 from Cincinnati*

Observation Lounge Car (Beverages)
Chicago to Cincinnati

Reclining Seat Coaches
Chicago to Cincinnati

Dining Service

October 1957

No. 3, James Whitcomb Riley, May 1957

Baggage Coach 286
Southern Sleeper 10-6 *Flint River*
  from Asheville, North Carolina from Southern Train No. 28
C&O Sleeper *City of Ashland*
  from Newport News, Virginia from C&O Train No. 41-1
Coach No. 3091
Coach No. 3066
Diner No. 691
Coach No. 3044
Tavern Lounge Observation No. 50

Note: This is a representative consist, and not a specific example.

Illinois Central No. 4036 was leased to the NYC through an arrangement originally designed to eliminate steam power from the Chicago-Cincinnati run since the IC had converted to diesels. Right behind the baggage cocach is the 10-6 which came off of the Southern in April 1956 view.

The *Riley* is leaving Cincinnati on March 26, 1967 with E8s Nos. 4087 and 4054. The train consists of a baggage car, two P-S coaches, a Budd diner (operating backwards) a C&O 10-6 sleeper from C&O 41-1, *The George Washington,* and another baggage car. Diners usually operated with the dining section forward to lessen smoke drifting into the dining section. By 1967, the NYC operated some trains without turning them at their destinations to save on switching costs. For the next run, engines were merely put on the opposite end and the train was hauled back to (in this case) Chicago.

On August 3, 1958, No. 3 carries an extra 10-6 (B&O) ahead of and in addition to the 10-6 from Newport News, Virginia off the C&O. Behind the C&O sleeper, is the 10-6 off the Southern. Power this morning consists of two consecutively numbered GP9s, 5941 and 5940 painted passenger gray. The train is seen leaving the Big Four tracks and going onto the Illinois Central which will take No. 3 to Chicago.

The *Empire State Express* carried 15 cars on June 27, 1948. The baggage-mail cars are noticeably absent.

Bob's Photos Collection

THE EMPIRE STATE EXPRESS
Nos. 50 and 51

One of the oldest (1891) named trains on the New York Central was the *Empire State Express*, completely re-equipped in 1941 with brand new stainless steel cars from the Budd Company. The *Empire State* was the premier day train between Cleveland and New York City and usually consisted of a mail/baggage car, a tavern lounge-parlor, six coaches, two parlor cars, two diners and one of the famous observation/lounge cars, *Theodore Roosevelt* and *Franklin Roosevelt*.

While mostly known as a New York-Buffalo express, the train originated and terminated at Cleveland Union Terminal with a section serving Detroit. Departures from New York and Cleveland were mid-morning, 8:00 A.M. from Grand Central Terminal and 9:50 A.M. from CUT. Stops were limited to 125th Street, Harmon, Albany, Schenectady, Utica, Syracuse, Rochester, Buffalo, then less limited west of Buffalo, stopping at Dunkirk, Westfield, Erie, and East Cleveland.

By 1956, the observation car operated between Buffalo and Grand Central Terminal only, as the train picked up cars for service from and to Detroit.

In October 1957, a westbound 10-6 was added at Buffalo for its run to St. Louis in No. 427, the *Gateway*, out of Cleveland. The switching of cars proved to be a burden and in October 1958, even the *Empire State Express* was not spared the reduction of status when the *Roosevelt* cars were removed from service, although for some years to follow one of the 58-70-series observation cars operated between New York and Albany for connecting service with the Delaware & Hudson Railway's *Laurentian* to Montreal. The observation cars lasted in this service until October 1964. Despite the changes in the consist, the schedules remained the same.

In 1960, NYC sold the four Budd-built named diners to a dealer who sold them to the Nacionales de Mexico. The observations had also been sold to NdeM in 1958. The baggage/lounge cars were sold to NdeM in 1961.

In 1964 and 1965, New York City hosted the World's Fair and in an attempt to provide a new and inexpensive-to-operate service for the large number of expected visitors, New York Central converted two of its 35-47-series Budd-built buffet/lounge cars to "Meal-A-Mat" cars, not much more than a rolling automat restaurant, to provide minimal food and beverage service on the *World's Fair Special*.

In October 1964, though, the *World's Fair Special* was discontinued and the two cars were briefly integrated into the *Empire State's* consist to supplement the regular dining service. The cars were not very popular, however, having all the charm, elegance and appeal of a soda machine. They were quickly removed and reassigned to Nos. 39 and 40, the *Cayuga*. In any event, regular dining service in the form of the Budd-built 450-467-series diners continued.

Sadly, the *Empire State Express* ended its long career as a nondescript coach train on December 2, 1967 and survived in an ethereal sense through Penn Central's and Amtrak's "Empire Service."

H. H. Harwood Jr.

Train 50 accelerates out of East Cleveland in December 1953 after its brief stop to pick up passengers. The catenary is still in place but the electric motors have ceased operations in Cleveland. The wires will soon be removed.

NYC No. 4002 and 4005 lead train No. 50, The *Empire State Express* at Lancaster, New York in April, 1949. The train is racin, at 60 MPH with 16 cars, including one of the assigned baggage RPO cars. The E7s have not yet been repainted into the nev lightning stripe scheme.

Lunch and dinner aboar the *Empire State Expres* could be pretty formal b today's standards. In th 1940s and 1950s, howeve this is how patrons aboar trains dressed and dined.

N.Y.C. to Spend $2,500,000 for Two New Streamliners

The New York Central will replace its present *Empire State Express*, which celebrates its 50th anniversary this year, with two new streamliners to cost between $2,000,000 and $2,500,000. The new equipment will be operated daily each way between New York, Buffalo and the Midwest.

For the new trains a total of 32 stainless steel cars have been ordered from the Edward G. Budd Manufacturing Company. Each of the two trains consist of the following cars:

    1 mail and mail-storage
    1 tavern-lounge-baggage
    3 parlor
    8 coaches
    1 observation-buffet

The new trains will be hauled by full-streamlined steam locomotives of the Hudson-type of a design similar to that of the locomotives now hauling the *Twentieth Century Limited*. Details as to builder of locomotives have not as yet been made available.

*(Excerpted from Railway Age
February 1, 1941)*

"When A Feller Needs A Friend"
... he finds one on the EMPIRE!

THE LADY IN THE TRIM UNIFORM is every youngster's friend aboard the **Empire State Express.** Every parent's too! As Central's Passenger Representative, she finds a hundred ways to make her hospitality helpful.

You'll see her getting little travelers acquainted ... helping to find lost toys ... pointing out the sights along the **Water Level Route.**

She'll help you find your reserved coach seat or parlor car chair. She'll take care of any telegrams you wish to send.

You'll hear her interpreting for passengers from overseas. For she's a college graduate, with a knowledge of at least one foreign language. And she'll make sure you know about the observation car (open to all passengers) and other features of this famous streamliner. She's there to help make your trip a "daylight delight" aboard the—

EMPIRE STATE EXPRESS

Daily. East and West, between New York, Buffalo,
Cleveland, Detroit. (Time Table 1 and 2)

The *Empire State Express*, led by freshly washed E8s 4049 and 4056 accelerate out of Rhinecliff with the all Budd consist associated with this train. Nos. 50 and 51 usually carried 13 to 15 cars. The 4049 has not yet undergone modifications since at this time, 1953, it had just arrived from the builder, EMD.

H. P. Stearns, J. W. Swanberg Collection

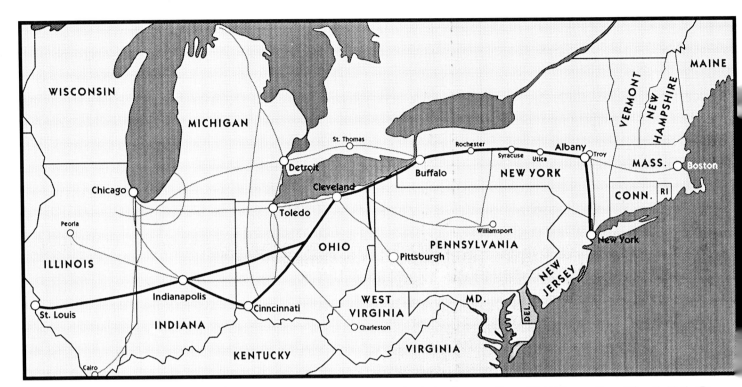

NEW YORK-CINCINNATI-ST. LOUIS

New York - Cincinnati - St. Louis

The *Southwestern Limited*, the *Knickerbocker*, the *Missourian* and the *Gateway*—these were the trains serving New York Central's important New York-St. Louis route over the Big Four (Cleveland, Cincinnati, Chicago and St. Louis Railroad or CCC & St L) which left NYC's New York-Chicago main line at Berea, Ohio, just west of Cleveland. Connecting service to the Southwest was provided at St. Louis at one of the nation's largest and most elegant terminals: St. Louis Union Station.

Trains leaving New York City for St. Louis followed NYC's main line up the Hudson River to Albany where they picked up cars from Boston, with stops at the major stations en route to Cleveland. At Collinwood Yard there would be a change to electric power again (until 1953) and after a stop at Cleveland Union Terminal where cars would be switched in or out, the train would continue west to Linndale where the electric power would be cut off and diesel power would take over. On the Big Four, passenger diesel power usually meant diesel units built by Fairbanks-Morse and General Motors (EMD) GP7 or GP9 steam generator equipped general purpose (hence "GP") locomotives.

At Berea, Ohio, the main line tracks split and headed southwest to Galion, Marion, Bellefontaine, Ohio; Muncie,

Anderson, Indianapolis, Terre Haute, Indiana; Paris, Mattoon, Pana, and Granite City, Illinois, among others.

At Galion, the main line split again for service to Cincinnati, the route traveled by the *Ohio State Limited*, Nos. 15 and 16. These trains carried cars to and from Boston for important connecting service from stations along the Boston and Albany main line.

Sleeping car service was provided in the form of both Pullman-Standard gray and Budd-built stainless steel cars of the 10-6, 6-bedroom/lounge car and 22-roomette variety with dining services provided en route, sometimes only between St. Louis and Indianapolis, or Cleveland, depending on the availability of cars and times when the dining cars would normally be patronized.

At Indianapolis, passengers could connect with trains to Chicago and points north, east, west, or south if they so desired. One could travel to Peoria, for example, via the trains of the Peoria and Eastern; or to Louisville via the Pennsylvania Railroad. One could also transfer to the trains of the Monon for service north of Indianapolis or make connections to the Baltimore and Ohio. The options were just simply amazing.

While NYC tried to make service between New York and St. Louis second to none, it was no match for the stiff competition with the Pennsylvania and its *Spirit of St. Louis Limited*, among others. The Pennsy's route was more direct and often faster. It wasn't until the early 1950s before the *Southwestern Limited* was fully stream-

Jay Williams

The eastbound *Missourian* makes a call on Schenectady, New York in October, 1961 EMD No. 4010 is paired with an Alco PB unit. While EMD and Alco freight units were not paired together on freight trains due to incompatible braking systems, passenger units did not have that problem.

lined and almost from the start, NYC found itself trying to play "catch up" adjusting schedules, services, etc. in an attempt to recapture their market share of a rapidly eroding traffic base.

The *Southwestern Limited*, endowed with a brand new Budd observation car similar in design to the *20th Century Limited's* "lookout" lounge (the *Southwestern Limited* was the *20th Century Limited's* Big Four counterpart in most respects), was one of the first trains to suffer the effects of service reductions. As time went on, the number of trains serving St. Louis would be cut back. The *Knickerbocker* and the *Southwestern Limited* would be the standard bearers of the St. Louis service through the 1950s and early 1960s.

Although the public sought out other modes of transport, NYC continued to provide daily coach, dining, and sleeping car service to the various cities along the Big Four route out of Cleveland with connecting and through service to other cities along its main lines. Passenger service between major points continued right up to the Penn Central merger in 1968.

J. David Ingles, Louis A. Marre Collection

This is the business side of St. Louis Union Station on December 19, 1965 as train No. 427 prepares to arrive. Trains arriving at St. Louis backed into the station. NYC trains operating over the Big Four were pulled by GP7s and GP9s, usually, after 1960.

OHIO STATE LIMITED

Nos. 15 and 16

The *Ohio State Limited* operated between New York and Cincinnati over the "Big Four" from Cleveland and carried coaches, a 6-double bedroom/lounge car, dining car(s) and 10-6 and 22-roomette sleepers between its main termini as well as between Boston-Cincinnati, Columbus-New York, Cleveland-New York, and Toronto-New York. Stops were made at Middletown, Dayton, Springfield, Columbus, Galion (Cleveland—to pick up or set off cars), Buffalo, Rochester, Syracuse, Utica, Schenectady, Albany, Poughkeepsie, and Harmon.

While New York Central offered different accommodations in overnight travel, the 10-roomette/6-double bedroom cars were the mainstay of the sleeping car service and once the standard cars had been retired, most of the overnight trains carried the Budd stainless steel or Pullman-Standard (gray) sleepers. Together, both Budd and Pullman-Standard delivered to NYC one hundred and thirty-seven 10-6s, more that any other type of lightweight sleeping car on the system.

In 1950, the *Ohio State Limited* carried mostly 10-6s. The trains were assigned two of the new Budd-built 5-double bedroom/lounge observation cars, *Plum Brook* and *Fall Brook* (identical cars ran on the *New England States*) although on occasion while one of these cars was being shopped, one of the Budd "lookout" observations built for the *Southwestern Limited* would be substituted. The eastbound train would leave Cincinnati at 4:00 P.M. for an 8:15 A.M. arrival in New York. Westbound No. 15 would also leave at 4:00 P.M. for an 8:30 A.M. arrival in Cincinnati.

In October 1956, the *Fall Brook* and *Plum Brook* observations were removed from the trains (they were sold to the Canadian Pacific three years later) and the schedule altered by an hour eastbound.

Through the early 1960s, little changed with the trains' consists and schedules. Cars were exchanged at Cleveland with No. 341, No. 2 and No. 312 for sleeper and coach service to and from St. Louis, Indianapolis, and Albany.

In 1961, No. 15 rated three 10-6s (New York-Cincinnati), a Buffalo-Cincinnati 10-6, a Cleveland-Cincinnati 22-roomette and a New York-Chicago 10-6 (in No. 27 from Buffalo). In April 1962, sleepercoach service was added between New York and Cincinnati.

By 1964, cutbacks became evident as sleeper service on No. 15 and 16 amounted to a New York-Cincinnati 10-6 and a sleepercoach; dining service; and coaches, although No. 16 picked up a Toronto 10-6 sleeper for New York at Buffalo and a 10-6 from St. Louis off No. 312 at Cleveland.

In October 1964, the westbound sleepercoach was

Sy Herring, Jay Williams Collection

E7s No. 4001 and 4005 approach Cincinnati with the *Ohio State Limited*, bereft of its Budd twin-unit diner set. A single Budd diner of the 447-449/691-699 series serves the coach patrons while a standard heavyweight diner serves the first class passengers. This may be one of two sections of the *Ohio State Limited*, evidenced by the flag by the fireman's window in this early 1950's view.

dropped and the eastbound sleepercoach offered between Cleveland and New York. A year later, sleeper-coach service was dropped altogether.

By April 1967, the *Ohio State Limited* still retained its consist of 10-6 sleeper, diner and coaches although on a longer schedule. By that November, No. 16 lost its proud name becoming a nondescript numbered and coach-only train running between Cincinnati and Cleveland, while No. 15 offered dining service Cleveland-Cincinnati and would make it into the last NYC timetable on December 3, 1967 as a pale shadow of its former self.

One of the most famous photos of NYC trains is of the westbound *20th Century* and the eastbound *Ohio State Limited* at Buffalo on November 28, 1948. E7 No. 4020 would be involved in a wreck in 1953 and return to service as an E8.

The westbound *Ohio State Limited* is seen at Oscawana, New York in August of 1950 with E7 No. 4020 in its as built form. Behind the Budd baggage/dormitory are two Pullman-Standard coaches, 6-double-bedroom lounge, twin-unit diner, five sleepers and 5-bedroom lounge observation.

While the passenger business was declining, the E units were occasionally paired with steam generator equipped GP7s or GP9s. In this case E7 No. 4027 and GP7 No. 5770 head a six car *Ohio State Limited* at Sharonville, Ohio on March 2, 1966. The 10-6 is running backwards (vestibule forward) and a grill-diner separates the car from the coaches. Such an arrangement will obviate turning the train at Cincinnati.

Louis A. Marre

The "*Century Inn,*" previously assigned to the *20th Century Limited*, was used on the *Southwestern Limited* after 1948. Passenger found the atmosphere relaxing and comfortable.

THE SOUTHWESTERN LIMITED

Nos. 11 and 12
Nos. 311 and 312

Of all the trains in the Great Steel Fleet, the *Southwestern Limited*, well equipped and well known, was not well patronized after being re-equipped in 1950. The train ran between New York and St. Louis over the Big Four route. It suffered competition from the Pennsylvania Railroad's *Spirit of St. Louis Limited* and *Penn Texas*, and to a minor extent, the Baltimore and Ohio's *National Limited*.

The *Southwestern Limited* had received some of the *20th Century Limited's* equipment along with the *Commodore Vanderbilt* from the 1938 train sets (remember, there were four 1938 *Century* train sets!) after the war. In addition to cars from New York City, Nos. 11 and 12 carried cars to and from Boston, Cleveland, Cincinnati, Toronto and Fort Monroe, Virginia (off train No. 1 *The George Washington* of the C&O at Cincinnati). Connecting service was made at St. Louis with the *Meteor*, the *Texas Special* and the *Texas Eagle* until October 1956, when these trains connected with the *Knickerbocker*.

In 1949, the trains had yet to be fully equipped with the new cars from Pullman and Budd. A review of No. 11's (westbound) consist in 1949 finds a 6-bedroom/lounge, three New York to St. Louis 10-6s, a 14-section heavyweight (HW) New York to St. Louis (Saturday only) Pullman; a New York to Cleveland 13-bedroom Pullman; a Boston to St. Louis 10-6, Boston to St. Louis 14-section (HW.) Pullman, a Boston to Cincinnati (except Saturday) 8-drawing room/2-compartment (HW.) Pullman, a Boston to Cleveland 10-6, Boston to Cleveland 18-roomette car, a Boston to Toronto 10-6; a 10-section/drawing room/2-double bedroom (HW) Pullman off the C&O train No. 1 at Cincinnati; a New York to St. Louis diner, New York to St. Louis coach, a Boston to St. Louis coach and a Cincinnati to St. Louis coach. As one can see, cars came from around the system and a lot of switching.

The 1949 train left St. Louis at 9:20 A.M. and arrived in New York City at 7:30 the next morning. No. 11 left

Louis A. Marre

GP7s and GP9s were generally the standard power on the Big Four. On September 2, 1963 Train No. 312, *The Southwestern Limited*, stops at Terre Haute, Indiana with a baggage car, two P-S coaches and a Budd 10-6.

Grand Central at 7:15 P.M. for a 3:50 P.M. arrival in St. Louis.

By June 1950, the trains had received the *Brook*-series observation cars but still carried a mix of standard and streamline equipment. This changed by 1953 when the trains were fully streamlined, but, because of the constant switching of cars, the observation cars were proving to be a problem (no less so for the occupants of its bedrooms) and by 1955 the cars were removed and served as back-up for the *20th Century Limited* and *Ohio State Limited* observations. (*Singing Brook* went to the Canadian Pacific in 1959. *Sunrise Brook* was retired in 1964 and sold.)

Between 1953 and 1956, the number of cars carried on Nos. 11 and 12 dropped dramatically. In 1955, in addition to the 6-double bedroom/lounge between New York and St. Louis, there were two New York-St. Louis 10-6s (from train 19-11 at Cleveland), two Boston cars (a 10-6 and a 22-roomette car from train 19-11 at Cleveland), a Boston-Toronto 10-5 Pullman and a Richmond, Virginia-St. Louis 10-6 from the C&O at Cincinnati in addition to coaches and dining service.

A year later, No. 11 carried the 6-bedroom/lounge, two New York-St. Louis 10-6 sleepers, a Boston 10-6 and the 10-6 off the C&O, a dining car and coaches. In October 1956 all sleeping cars were gone with a westbound departure from New York City eliminated with Nos. 11 and 12 originating and terminating in Cleveland and listing only dining service (a "thrift grill") and coaches between Cleveland and St. Louis.

Sleeper service was restored in another schedule change in October 1957 when No. 11, originating in Cleveland, picked up a 10-6 from New York from No. 57, the *Cleveland Limited*. No. 12 provided a 6-double bedroom/lounge and 10-6s to New York and Boston on the *Cleveland Limited* and *New England States*, respectively, through Cleveland, with dining service from St. Louis to Cleveland and coaches.

In the 1958 schedule change, Nos. 11 and 12 became Nos. 311 and 312, originating in Cleveland, providing 10-6 sleeper service between New York and St. Louis and to Boston via connections at Cleveland.

In 1959, No. 311 disappeared from the timetable leaving only No. 312 eastbound to Cleveland from St. Louis but with 10-6 sleeper service to New York City and Boston in Nos. 16 and 28, respectively. The Boston 10-6 was dropped in October with an Indianapolis-to-New York 10-6 added.

The *Southwestern Limited* last appeared in the October 30, 1966 timetable listing a St. Louis to New York 10-6, a buffet lounge (Indianapolis to Cleveland) and through-coaches to New York in the *New England States* at Cleveland to No. 54 at Albany, often a five car train, including the baggage car, drawn by two GP9s.

No. 11—THE SOUTHWESTERN—DAILY—WESTBOUND
Sleeping Car
 New York to St. Louis, Ex. Sat. (10 Roomette-6 Double Bedroom)—From No. 7 at Cleveland—Will not run Nov. 28, 29; Dec. 22, 23, 24, 29, 30 or 31
Diner Lounge
 Cleveland to St. Louis
Coaches
 New York to St. Louis (Ex. Sat.)—From No. 57 at Cleveland—Will not run Nov. 28, 29; Dec. 22, 23, 24, 29, 30 or 31
 Cleveland to St. Louis

No. 12—THE SOUTHWESTERN—DAILY—EASTBOUND
Lounge Sleeping Car
 St. Louis to New York (6 Double Bedroom-Beverages)—In No. 58 from Cleveland, Ex. Sat. On Saturdays will operate in No. 28-16 from Cleveland to New York
Sleeping Car
 St. Louis to New York (Ex. Sat.) (10 Roomette-6 Double Bedroom)—In No. 58 from Cleveland
 St. Louis to New York (10 Roomette-6 Double Bedroom)—In No. 58 from Cleveland, Ex. Sat. On Saturdays will operate in No. 28-16 from Cleveland to New York
 St. Louis to Boston (10 Roomette-6 Double Bedroom)—In No. 28 from Cleveland
Dining Service
 St. Louis to Cleveland
Coaches
 St. Louis to New York—In No. 58 from Cleveland. On Saturdays will operate in No. 28-16 from Cleveland to New York
 St. Louis to Cleveland

By October 1957, service on the *Southwest Limited* was winding down. It seems it was being rationed.

No. 12—THE SOUTHWESTERN—DAILY—EASTBOUND
Lounge Sleeping Car
 St. Louis to New York (6 Double Bedroom-Beverages)—In No. 58 from Cleveland, Ex. Sat. On Saturdays will operate in No. 28-16 from Cleveland to New York
Sleeping Car
 St. Louis to New York (Ex. Sat.) (10 Roomette-6 Double Bedroom)—In No. 58 from Cleveland
 St. Louis to New York (10 Roomette-6 Double Bedroom)—In No. 58 from Cleveland, Ex. Sat. On Saturdays will operate in No. 28-16 from Cleveland to New York
 St. Louis to Boston (10 Roomette-6 Double Bedroom)—In No. 28 from Cleveland
Dining Service
 St. Louis to Cleveland
Coaches
 St. Louis to New York—In No. 58 from Cleveland. On Saturdays will operate in No. 28-16 from Cleveland to New York
 St. Louis to Cleveland

No. 11—THE SOUTHWESTERN—DAILY—WESTBOUND
Sleeping Car
 New York to St. Louis, Ex. Sat. (10 Roomette-6 Double Bedroom)—From No. 7 at Cleveland—Will not run Nov. 28, 29; Dec. 22, 23, 24, 29, 30 or 31
Diner Lounge
 Cleveland to St. Louis
Coaches
 New York to St. Louis (Ex. Sat.)—From No. 57 at Cleveland—Will not run Nov. 28, 29; Dec. 22, 23, 24, 29, 30 or 31
 Cleveland to St. Louis

Sy Herring, Jay Williams Collection

he *Southwestern Limited* is pulling into its stop at Bellefontaine, Ohio in 1955. The *Southwestern* still carries an impressive con-
st of coaches and sleepers, including a heavyweight car or two. Fluctuations in demand necessitated the use of whatever
quipment might be on hand at various terminals across the system.

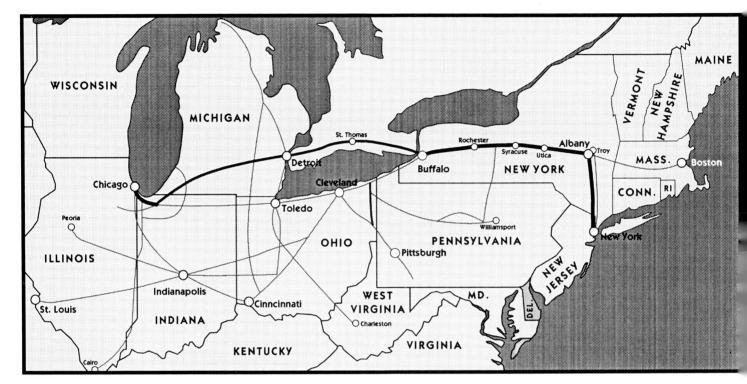

CHICAGO-NEW YORK VIA DETROIT

CHICAGO-NEW YORK

Via Detroit (and Canada)

Among the most heavily traveled routes on New York Central was the Chicago-New York main line over the Michigan Central via Detroit. Complementing the *Mercury* trains and secondary trains serving Detroit, there were through trains leaving the east-west main line at Porter, Indiana, just west of Chesterton, joining it again just west of Buffalo Central Terminal.

In addition to the *Wolverine*, trains such as the *New York Special*, the *Detroiter*, the *Niagara* and the *North Shore Limited* augmented the Chicago-Detroit corridor service and provided sleeping car accommodations to points east and west as well as service to Cincinnati via Toledo.

After leaving Englewood on Chicago's south side, trains made stops at Michigan City, Indiana; Niles, Kalamazoo, Battle Creek, Albion, Jackson, Ann Arbor, Detroit, Michigan; Windsor and London, Ontario; Niagara Falls and Buffalo eastbound and in reverse on the westbound. At Buffalo, there was connecting service to other points on the system, such as to the Pittsburgh and Lake Erie Railroad and to the Toronto, Hamilton, and Buffalo Railway which was jointly owned by NYC and the Canadian Pacific Railway.

At Detroit, service to northern Michigan began to such places as Saginaw and Bay City and (via Jackson) to Grand Rapids. Sleeping car service was provided in the form of a 10-6 Bay City to New York City sleeper in No. 44, the *New York Special*, eastbound, and in No. 47 the *Detroiter*, westbound.

The Michigan Central trains left from the Illinois Central's lake front Central Station before being moved over to La Salle Street Station beginning in the late 1940s,

a consolidation which simplified departures for those who might be otherwise confused by the two points of departure in Chicago. At that time, NYC made a point to indicate in its timetables which trains traveling via Detroit would originate and terminate in either station. In fact, up until the mid-1950s, the trains leaving and terminating at Central Station commanded their own separate timetables in the System Form 1001.

With the elimination of the *Detroiter's* all-Pullman service and the comprehensive schedule and service revisions in the late 1950s, service over the Michigan Central was only slightly tarnished. It continued to be a vital part of NYC's passenger fleet operations, and in fact, the Detroit routing would remain active through the 1960s until the merger of the two northeastern giants—the New York Central and the Pennsylvania Railroads.

No. 44—NEW YORK SPECIAL—DAILY—EASTBOUND

Lounge Sleeping Cars
Niagara Falls to New York, Ex. Sat. (6 Double Bedroom-Buffet)—From No. 246 at Buffalo—*will not operate Nov. 28, 29; Dec. 22, 23, 24, 29, 30 or 31*

Sleeping Cars
Chicago to New York (10 Roomette-6 Double Bedroom)
Chicago to Boston (10 Roomette-6 Double Bedroom)—*In No. 46 from Buffalo*
Detroit to New York (10 Roomette-5 Double Bedroom)—*In No. 16 from Buffalo*
Detroit to New York (12 Double Bedroom)
Detroit to New York, Ex. Sat. (22 Roomette)
Detroit to Boston, Ex. Sat. (10 Roomette-6 Double Bedroom)—*In No. 46 from Buffalo—will not operate Nov. 28, 29; Dec. 22, 23, 24, 25, 29, 30, 31 or April 4*
Niagara Falls to New York (10 Roomette-5 Double Bedroom)—*From No. 246 at Buffalo*
Buffalo to New York, Sat. only (10 Roomette-6 Double Bedroom)
Syracuse to New York (10 Roomette-6 Double Bedroom)
Syracuse to New York, Ex. Sat. Night-Sun. Morn. (22 Roomette)—*Will not operate A. M. of Nov. 29, 30; Dec. 23, 24, 25, 30, 31 or Jan. 1*
Rochester to New York, Ex. Sat. (10 Roomette-5 Double Bedroom)—*From Auburn Road No. 18-8 at Syracuse—Will not run a. m.'s of Nov. 29, 30; Dec. 23, 24, 25, 30, 31 or Jan. 1*
Massena to New York via Watertown (10 Roomette-5 Double Bedroom)—*From St. Law. Div. No. 8-808 at Syracuse*

Dining Service
Chicago to Detroit—Diner Lounge
Detroit to Buffalo

Coaches
Chicago to New York (Reclining Seat)

No. 47—THE DETROITER—EX. SAT.—WESTBOUND
Will not run Nov. 28, 29; Dec. 22, 23, 24, 25, 29, 30, 31 or April 4

Lounge Sleeping Cars
New York to Detroit (6 Double Bedroom-Beverages)

Sleeping Cars
New York to Detroit (4 Comp.-4 Double Bedroom-2 D. R.)
New York to Detroit (12 Double Bedroom)—Three
New York to Detroit (22 Roomette)—Two
Boston to Detroit (10 Roomette-6 Double Bedroom)—*From No. 35 at Albany*
Buffalo to Detroit (22 Roomette)

Dining Service

Reclining Seat Coach
New York to Detroit—All Seats Reserved—Porter Service

No. 48—THE DETROITER—EX. SAT.—EASTBOUND

Lounge Sleeping Cars
Detroit to New York (6 Double Bedroom-Beverages)

Sleeping Cars
Detroit to New York (4 Comp.-4 Double Bedroom-2 D. R.)
Detroit to New York (12 Double Bedroom)—Two
Detroit to New York (22 Roomette)

Dining Service

Reclining Seat Coach
Detroit to New York—All Seats Reserved—Porter Service

No. 337—NORTHBOUND
No. 338—SOUTHBOUND
THE NORTHERNER—DAILY

Sleeping Car
Detroit and Mackinaw City (17 Roomette)

Coach
Detroit and Mackinaw City

These three sections from late 1957 Form 1001 timetables show the accommodations available. On the table above, one of the 1938 17 roomette cars was assigned to provide sleeper service to Mackinaw City from Detroit.

The interior of the RDC was utilitarian - no frills. NYC operated its Beeliners over those stretches where "passenger miles" were low and service could be provided with reduced costs. Quite often, service was mandated by state regulatory agencies and the Beeliners could reduce losses over an engine drawn train.

NYCSHS Collection

Beeliner M-498 is at Lansing, Michigan on its Bay City-Jackson run during July of 1959. M-498 is an RDC-3 (Baggage/Mail/Coach) and its mail contract helped defray the operating costs, since the coach appears to be empty.

Both: Jerry Pinkepank, Louis A. Marre Collection

By 1960, the RDC gained high visibility zebra stripes with and orange stripe for grade crossing safety. M-499 i seen at Mackinav City in Augus 1960. The RDC could be operate in either direction thus saving on turning facilities.

Mail and express Train No. 13 is about to enter the Detroit River Tunnel at Windsor, Ontario on September 8, 1966. Railway Express and Flexivans make up a large portion of the train.

J. David Ingles, Collection of Louis A. Marre

THE WOLVERINE

Nos. 8 and 17

The *Wolverine* operated between Chicago and New York by way of the Michigan Central route through Detroit to Buffalo. While it was considered one of the crack limiteds over the Chicago-to-New York route, via Detroit, it also carried cars for other trains to provide service across the system. It typically left Chicago about 2:00 P.M. with a 9:30 A.M. arrival in New York City, and a 5:15 P.M. departure from New York with an 11:00 A.M. arrival in Chicago.

Nos. 8 and 17 carried a combination of standard and streamline equipment in 1947, but mostly standard. By 1950, No. 8 still carried a 12-section/1-drawing room (HW) Pullman which was transferred at Albany to No. 98, the *Paul Revere*, for the trip through the Berkshires to Boston. Also in 1950 it gained an observation parlor car operating west of Detroit.

The 1950 timetable notes that the train left from La Salle Street Station, as it was common for the trains using the Michigan Central to leave from the Illinois Central's waterfront Central Station. Then in 1952 No. 8 began carrying a 10-roomette/6-double bedroom car from San Francisco via the Overland Route (Chicago & North Western-until October 1957, then briefly Milwaukee/Union Pacific until February 1958).

In 1953, a tavern lounge to Detroit was added and in 1955 it picked up sleepers from Cincinnati (to Boston) at Buffalo; St. Louis (to Boston) at Buffalo; and Pittsburgh (to Massena, New York) at Buffalo switched out at Syracuse (an 8-section/4- double bedroom Pullman). Coaches from St. Louis to Boston were also picked up at Buffalo from the combined *Southwestern Limited/Ohio State Limited* and turned over to the *Paul Revere* at Albany.

In 1957, the *Wolverine* lost its observation car but still sported two 10-6s and a 22-roomette car with Saturday-only Detroit to New York sleeper service in the form of a 22-roomette and a 12-double bedroom duo.

In 1958, the Detroit cars were a daily service with the addition of one of the 1938-40 vintage 4-compartment/4 double bedroom/2-drawing room cars (4-4-2). The train also began carrying one of the twin dining car sets off the *20th Century Limited*, made surplus by the combination of the *20th Century Limited* and the *Commodore Vanderbilt*, until they were withdrawn in 1960 these car also saw service on the *Twilight Limited*.

In October 1958, No. 8 was combined with the *Detroiter* and listed 10 sleepers including a Saturday night-only Rochester to New York 10-6. The combination was short lived. By April 1959 the *Wolverine* ran on it own schedule with a 2:00 P.M. departure from La Sall Street with arrival at Grand Central Terminal at 9:00 A.M.

The westbound *Wolverine*, No. 17, operated much th same way as its eastbound counterpart although it le Grand Central Terminal at 6:30 P.M. for an arrival i Chicago La Salle Street at 1:30 P.M.

In 1962, the *Wolverines* began carrying the ne sleepercoaches converted by Budd from the 22-roomett

E7 No. 4004, one of the first passenger locomotives delivered to NYC in 1945 from EMC, leads E8 No. 4043 on Train No. 8, The *Wolverine*, at Crugers, New York. The Hancock air whistle had a nice steam whistle quality to it, but only 4004, 4006 and several RS-2s were equipped with it. NYC's Grand Central neighbor (New Haven) used them almost exclusively.

J. W. Swanberg

Harbor-series cars between Detroit and New York. In 1963 the train advertised a parlor car (sleeper-as-parlor) between Chicago and Detroit, a 10-6 between Chicago and New York, a 10-6 between Detroit and New York, a 10-6 between Detroit and Boston (in the *New England States* east of Buffalo) and two Toronto to New York 10-6s.

By April 1964, the observation parlor car was back between Chicago and Detroit, but gone by October. The *Wolverine's* sleeper service from Toronto was also discontinued. The consist remained virtually unchanged until November 1967 when Nos. 8 and 17 lost the Detroit-New York sleepers, but regained a 10-6 between Toronto and New York. One month later Nos. 8 and 17 became part of the remnant trains just prior to the Penn Central merger.

THE DETROITER (Except Saturday)
Nos. 47 and 48

Not all of New York Central's streamliners were outfitted with observation cars, but a few, even in 1950, carried only sleepers and were listed as Pullman Cars only; no coach passengers carried." In 1950, when most of the Pullman-Standard and Budd cars had arrived, Nos. 47 and 48 carried two 6-bedroom/lounge cars, two 4-4-2s, three 12-double bedroom cars, two 22-roomette cars, and a Bay City, Michigan 10-6 at Detroit. The *Detroiter*, in company with the *20th Century Limited* and *Commodore Vanderbilt*, was prestigious—it was all gray (there were only three trains which were assigned all gray equipment—truly, "Pullman Cars only.)"

With an early evening departure from Detroit at 7:00 P.M., it would arrive by the subterranean platforms of Grand Central Terminal 7:30 the next morning with stops only at Buffalo, Syracuse, and Albany for crew changes and a scheduled stop at Harmon. It was the most limited of the limiteds.

Even in early April 1956, the *Detroiter's* stature as an all-Pullman streamliner was untarnished. Westbound, at Buffalo it would pick up a Boston-Detroit 6-double bedroom/lounge car and a Boston-Detroit 10-6 from No. 33, the *New England Wolverine*, and a Hoboken-Detroit 6-section/6-double bedroom (H.W.) car from Delaware, Lackawanna and Western No. 5, the *Twilight*, as well as a 6- double bedroom/lounge car which was cut out at Buffalo for service to Cleveland in No. 221. These cars were in addition to the two 6-bedroom/lounge cars, two 4-4-2s, a 12-double bedroom, two 13-double bedroom cars, a 10-6, two 22-roomette cars and dining cars.

In April 1956, however, the service changed with the addition of coaches, but in all other respects the train was the same, although Albany, Syracuse, and Buffalo were new scheduled stops.

In October 1958, the *Detroiter* still listed a full complement of sleeping equipment which exemplified the types of cars the New York Central operated: an *Imperial* series (4-4-2) Pullman, two 12-double bedroom *Port* series cars, a 10-6, two 22-roomette cars, a 6-double bedroom/lounge car and a 13-double bedroom *County* series Pullman. In April 1959, though, the *Detroiter* was gone with overnight service on essentially the same schedule provided by the *Wolverine*.

Mayor Daley's urban renewal project is still a few years away, but already the real estate south of La Salle Street Station is thinning out. The airline strike has swelled No. 8's consist on August 8, 1966.

Theodore Shrady

As the new Budd and Pullman-Standard cars arrived, NYC wasted no time employing them in their trains. Budd and P-S coaches and diner behind the locomotives; standard heavyweight sleepers and diner can be seen just ahead of the eastbound *Wolverine's* parlor observation in this scene at Englewood, Illinois in 1949.

No. 8, The Wolverine, April 1955

Baggage 8724 (Chicago-New York)
Baggage/dormitory 8961 (Chicago-New York)
Coach No. 2918   (Chicago-New York)
Coach No. 2935   (Chicago-New York)
Coach No. 2936   (Chicago-New York)
Twin-unit diner No. 470-411   (Chicago-New York)
Sleeper 22-roomette *Casco Bay* (Chicago-New York)
Sleeper 10-6 *Hudson River*   (Chicago-New York)
Sleeper 10-6 *Detroit River*   (Chicago-New York)
6-bedroom/lounge *Big Moose Lake*   (Chicago-New York)
Tavern lounge coach 47   (Chicago-New York)
Observation parlor 61   (Chicago-Detroit)
12-bedroom (Saturday only) (Detroit-New York) Port of Oswego
10-6 *Beaver River* (Detroit-New York)
10-6 *Klamath Valley* (Detroit-Albany) to Boston in No. 78
12 section D.R. *Albany* (Sunday only) (Detroit-Buffalo) to Albany in No. 24
10-6 *Niantic River* (from St. Louis to Buffalo in No. 16) in No. 78 from Albany to Boston
10-6 *Missouri Valley* (from Cincinnati in No. 16; in No. 78 from Albany to Boston
8 sct/4-bdrm *Emerald Hill* (from P&LE No. 33/NYC 284 from Pittsburgh)
(In NYC No. 7-707 to Massena via Watertown, New York.)

Note: This is a representative consist, and not a specific example.

NEW YORK CENTRAL SYSTEM

The *Interstate Express*, Train No. 46 departs its station stop at Newtonville, Massachusetts bound for Boston on December 30, 1950. Mohawk No. 3024 pulls a train mixed with prewar streamlined, standard equipment and a couple of postwar cars.

Train No. 27 at Englewood in August 1949 is led by a trio of F3s, bought for use on the *New England States* when the diesel-hungry NYC experimented with different power arrangements. The four coaches are from Pullman-Standard, not the usual assignment for the normally all-Budd train. A 44-seat diner is just behind those coaches.

THE B&A

Chicago-Detroit-St. Louis-Boston

While many associate NYC with high-speed trains serving Chicago and New York, equally important were those trains which left the main line across the Hudson River from Albany at Rensselaer and headed upgrade to Post Road Crossing where they headed through the Berkshires of Massachusetts for a rendezvous with the bumperposts at Boston's venerable South Station. Trains like the *New England States*, the *Berkshire*, the *Iroquois*, the *Paul Revere*, the *Interstate Express* and the Boston sections of the *Wolverine*, *Chicagoan* and the *Lake Shore Limited* offered the long distance passenger of 1948 a variety of comfortable departures and accommodations designed to fit any budget.

The Boston and Albany Railroad was operated by New York Central under the terms of a long-term lease agreement which expired on April 3, 1961 with the merger of the two companies. It operated commuter trains out of South Station and offered trains to Albany and beyond with sleeping cars of all types being ferried in the other numerous trains of the Great Steel Fleet. From Boston, a person could travel to any point on the New York Central System and connect at any of the many terminals for thousands of other destinations throughout the country.

The *Paul Revere*, for example, carried sleeping cars from the *Southwestern Limited* to and from St. Louis via a connection at Albany. The *New England States*, originally a through train, eventually would pick up cars from the *Southwestern Limited*, after the elimination of the *Paul Revere*, and from the *Wolverine* at Buffalo. The *Interstate Express* carried cars from Detroit, Toronto and Montreal, Lake Placid, Massena (N.Y.), Buffalo, and Pittsburgh.

The Boston and Albany was a twisting and winding railroad which followed and crossed over rivers and streams and which offered its many patrons grand terminals in cities such as Boston, Worcester, Springfield, and Pittsfield, Massachusetts. Many of its freight houses carried a New York Central herald, but in huge letters, as if one had to be reminded, was the name, "Boston and Albany Railroad."

The B&A, as it is still known, powered its passenger trains with locomotives built by the American Locomotive Company (ALCO), EMD, Fairbanks-Morse, and Baldwin Locomotive Works, later Baldwin-Lima-Hamilton. The passenger engines from ALCO were in the form of the regal PAs and steam generator equipped RS2s and RS3s; passenger units from F-M were in the form of their well-known C-Liner series and the rather unreliable "Gravel Gerties" from Baldwin. The F-M and Baldwin units didn't stand up to the grueling grades of the B&A, but the ALCO engines seemed best suited for the route and, along with the EMD E7 and E8 engines, became the mainstay of the B&A passenger fleet power pool in the 1950s.

Due to the hilly terrain, top speed on the B&A was 50 mph in only a few locations, but for most of the road, speed was restricted to 40 mph because of the many curves. While it was common to see two PAs coupled together or perhaps an EMD E-unit with a trailing PA, three-unit sets of EMD Es were a common sight when leading the *New England States*.

In the wake of the arrival of the new cars, trains made stops at Pittsfield, Springfield, Worcester, and Framingham before arriving at Back Bay Station, the last stop before South Station. When the new rail diesel cars (RDC) from Budd started arriving in the mid-1950s, the "Beeliners" provided intermediate passenger service to supplement the diesel drawn trains.

The Boston and Albany passenger service played an important role in the New York Central's passenger market. The *New England States* would last to carry on in number only after the demise of the *20th Century Limited*. Passenger service west of Springfield, Massachusetts was terminated in mid-1971. Penn Central lost no time tearing out the rails between Rensselaer and Post Road Crossing. There was such great demands that the service be reinstated, however, the tracks had to be put back in place after passenger service resumed in the mid-1970s.

NYC Photo, J. W. Swanberg Collection

The *New England States* is at Russell, Massachusetts "in service" on August 14, 1952. The first coach has not been repainted from its pre-war green scheme.

The observation lounge of *Babbling Brook* was a great place to read, work, play cars or just view the ever changing vista aboard the New England States. The train has left Boston and before nightfall will be coiling thru the Berkshires.

Two Alco PA-1s lead the "pullman cars only" all Budd No. 27 at Riverside, Massachusetts, just outside of Boston in 1949.

THE NEW ENGLAND STATES
Nos. 27 and 28

Nos. 27 and 28 had their origins in the Boston section of the pre-1938 *20th Century Limited* and as such was the premier train on the Boston and Albany Railroad and the flagship of the New York Central's Boston/Chicago service which also included the *Paul Revere*, the *New England Wolverine*, the *Berkshire*, and the *Interstate Express*. Outfitted with all new stainless steel equipment from Budd in late 1949, it began the new streamline era as an all-room Pullman train carrying forth the all-sleeping-car tradition associated with this train's heritage.

By early 1950, the *New England States* boasted a 5-bedroom/lounge observation (*Bonnie Brook* and *Babbling Brook*), a 6-bedroom/lounge car, five 10-6s, a twin-unit diner, with a lounge in the kitchen car, and for the first time, reclining seat coaches, usually three or four, and one of the new Budd dormitory/baggage cars.

The train offered an early afternoon departure from Chicago (2:40 P.M. in 1950) and Boston (2:00 P.M.) for arrivals at 9:30 A.M. in Boston and 7:40 A.M. in Chicago.

For the next 17 years the departures didn't deviate by more than a couple hours eastbound and an hour westbound with the schedules lengthened on both ends as service to and from other cities was added.

Typically, in the early 1950s No. 28 left Chicago at 2:00 P.M. with stops at Englewood, Gary, South Bend, Elkhart, Toledo, Buffalo, Pittsfield, Springfield, Worcester, Framingham, Newtonville, and Boston. No. 27 left Boston at 2:30 P.M. making the stops above in reverse, but adding Schenectady and Syracuse.

In 1956, both Nos. 27 and 28 carried their standard consists, a 5-bedroom lounge observation, four 10-6s, the twin-unit diner set, a lounge/coach and reclining seat coaches in addition to the baggage/dormitory car, with No. 27 carrying in addition a Buffalo to Chicago 10-6.

By October 1956, the familiar 5-double bedroom *Brook*-series observation cars disappeared becoming a victim of the cost of switching cars at intermediate points along with the realignment of service and schedules. At Buffalo, for example, No. 27 delivered a Boston-Chicago 10-6 and a Boston to Detroit 10-6 to the westbound *Wolverine*; a Boston-to-Pittsburgh 10-6 to No. 279 for delivery to the Pittsburgh and Lake Erie; an Albany-to

NYC Photo, Collection of Jack Swanberg

Posed for the company photographer at South Spencer, Massachusetts. The *New England States* is equipped with *Babbling Brook* a 5 double-bedroom lounge, on June 8, 1949.

Pittsburgh 10-5; and at Toledo, picked up a C&O 10-6 from Charlottesville, Virginia, to Chicago. No. 28 carried the return portions except for the Albany car.

The *New England States*, along with the *20th Century Limited*, received the first of four new Budd-built 24-roomette/8-double bedroom sleepercoaches in October 1959, each train carrying one. In April 1962, the newly arrived rebuilt sleepercoaches (former 22-roomette *Harbor*-series cars) from Budd were placed in service and assigned one each to Nos. 27 and 28, the four 24-8s going to the *20th Century Limited*, two carried in each train set.

A dramatic change occurred in October 1961 when Number 2, the *Pacemaker*, merged with No. 28 eastbound to be separated at Cleveland, later (1962) at Buffalo. In 1963, No. 27 left Boston at 3:15 P.M. for a 9:15 A.M. arrival in Chicago; No. 28 left Chicago at 4:05 P.M., combined with No. 2, the *Pacemaker*.

By 1964, No. 2 had been reduced to a 6-bedroom/lounge car from Cleveland to New York and coaches out of Chicago cut ahead or behind the Boston cars. This charade ceased effective April 24, 1966.

In April 1965, Nos. 27 and 28 carried one 10-6 each. In October, they briefly carried a 12-bedroom car and a Budd 22-roomette car in an attempt to better utilize the equipment on hand. The following April, however, both trains had two 10-6s restored to the consists as sale of the passenger cars continued.

The *New England States* outlived the *20th Century Limited*, in a sense, and for a brief time (a month—November 1967) was combined with Nos. 25 and 26 west of Buffalo. It lost its name with the December 3, 1967 change, but survives in spirit today in the form of Amtrak's *Lake Shore Limited*.

S. K. Bolton Photo, H. H. Harwood Collection

The two Alcos are accelerating fast and rolling out a cloud of typical black smoke. As the *New England States* races west through Palmer, Massachusetts in the summer of 1951. The (almost) all Budd train will be making a short station stop at Springfield, just about 15 miles away.

CHICAGO-NEW YORK

The pride of the NYC was its east-west main line between Chicago and New York City over the "Water Level Route." The term "water level" was meant to convey the notion of a straight and smooth ride and if that wasn't enough, it added the phrase "you can sleep" to its advertising. This was an innuendo directed at its competition, the Pennsylvania, with its many curves and mountainous grades.

One of the hallmarks of NYC was its high-speed four-track main line from New York City to Buffalo and beyond. NYC was an enormous railroad and never did anything in a small way. Not only could the patron enjoy the beautiful scenery along the Hudson River and through the Mohawk Valley, but the journey would be smooth and relaxing. The passenger couldn't help but be impressed with the physical plant and operations - they were on a grand scale which was first-rate. All the while, gliding along at 80 mph, the passenger was feted in a manner consistent with an opulent grand hotel - a rolling opulent grand hotel—replete with an ever changing vista.

In 1950, NYC sent westbound to Chicago from Grand Central Terminal seven limiteds: the *North Shore Limited* (via Detroit) at 12:00pm; the "Coach only" *Pacemaker*, combined with the "Pullman Cars only" *Advance Commodore Limited* at 3:00pm; the *Commodore Vanderbilt* ("Pullman Cars only") at 4:30pm; the *20th Century Limited* ("Pullman Cars only") at 5:00pm; the *Wolverine* (via Detroit) at 6:00 pm; the *Lake Shore Limited* at 6:15pm; and the *Chicagoan* at 11:00pm.

From Chicago, eastbound, nine trains departed the platforms of La Salle Street and Central Station for New York City; the *New York Special* (Central Station via Detroit) at 9:45 am; the *Fifth Avenue Special* (La Salle Street) at 12:30pm; the *Wolverine* (La Salle Street via Detroit) at 2:40pm; the *Commodore Vanderbilt* ("Pullman Cars only," - La Salle Street) at 3:00pm; the *Pacemaker* ("Coach only") combined with the *Commodore II* ("Pullman Cars only") at 3:20pm; the *20th Century Limited* ("Pullman Cars only") at 4:00pm; the Mohawk at 4:40pm; the *Lake Shore Limited* at 6:15 pm; and the *Chicagoan* at 11:00pm.

In 1951, the *"Commodore II"* would become the *Advance Commodore Vanderbilt*, still combined with the *Pacemaker* both eastbound and westbound. The combining of trains would become an increasing practice in an attempt to reduce operating costs while still maintaining a high level of service.

A typical limited traveling east would make stops at Englewood, Gary, South Bend, Elkhart, Toledo, Sandusky, Elyria, Linndale (for the change of power until 1953), Cleveland, East Cleveland, Collinwood (power change), Erie, Buffalo, Rochester, Syracuse, Rome, Utica, Schenectady Albany, and Harmon where all trains entering New York changed over to electric power before the final dash to Grand Central Terminal.

Major cross-platform connections to other railroads could be made at Toledo with the Baltimore and Ohio; at Cleveland with the Nickel Plate (New York, Chicago and St. Louis Railroad) and the Erie; at Buffalo with the Pennsylvania Railroad and the Delaware Lackawanna & Western; and at Albany with the Delaware and Hudson.

In 1948, and throughout the early 1950s, several of the through trains made very few stops. For example, the combined *Pacemaker* and *Advance Commodore Vanderbilt* made scheduled stops at Englewood, Gary, South Bend, Elkhart, Toledo, Linndale, and Cleveland before its next one at Harmon the following morning. Actually, stops were made to change crews and to service engines and cars at Buffalo, Syracuse and Albany. These stops were not listed in the public timetable since passengers could not get on or off at these locations.

By 1953, NYC had purchased enough new diesel locomotives to power most of its passenger trains. With the conversion to diesel power, slowly the famous steam locomotives of New York Central, the Mohawks, the Hudsons and even the newest steam locomotives, the Niagaras, were cycled through to secondary assignments before scrapping. They were sequestered, in a sense, to

Elmer Trealor, Jay Williams Collectio

The *Iroquois*, Train No. 35 (Boston-Chicago) is being serviced at Toledo's new Central Terminal on May 3, 1950. Niagara No. 6001 and the other 24 of its clas had but just a few short years of service left.

the lines west of Cleveland and the routes of the Big Four.

One could witness all types of the newest passenger power from the four locomotive builders who catered to NYC. Most of the crack limiteds, such as the *20th Century Limited*, *Commodore Vanderbilt* and the *Pacemaker* rated EMD E7s and E8s in pairs, although the *20th Century Limited* usually rated three E-units. The 13 NYC ALCO PAs were usually assigned to New York and New England trains since they were based and serviced out of Harmon and Collinwood. The secondary trains were usually led by Fairbanks-Morse units and those few which had been purchased from Baldwin. In time, however, the passenger fleet would become the domain of the EMD units as the engines from the other builders proved to be troublesome and moves were made to cut operating costs and streamline servicing and maintenance.

The Chicago-New York name trains offered the comforts of the twin-unit diners, lounges and sleeping cars, carrying anywhere from 13 to 20 cars in each, depending upon traffic. Trains had a maximum speed restriction of 85 mph on the main line and schedules were timed to provide as close to a 16-hour transit between the two cities as possible.

In 1948, new train services were heralded as though a new oceanic liner was being sent forth on its maiden voyage and often with eye cast in the direction of Chicago's Union or New York's Penn Station. When NYC received four new leased 24-roomette/8-bedroom "sleepercoaches," (Nos. 10800-10803) in 1959 from the Budd Company for use on the *20th Century Limited* and the *New England States*, the new cars were promoted primarily in its timetables and brochures. The new economy sleeping car service was expected to draw back passenger traffic by making sleeping car travel more affordable.

Rail vs. Air in Toledo

A favorite pastime in Toledo, Ohio, (population: 330,000) used to be criticizing its ancient Union Station. Built in 1886, the passenger facility was owned by New York Central but used by B&O, C&O and Wabash. Civic wrath reached such a pitch that a local businessman erected a billboard which read DON'T JUDGE TOLEDO BY ITS UNION STATION. Central finally capitulated after the war despite the fact that it was piling up bigger and bigger passenger deficits. The road spent 5 million dollars of its own money to erect a brand-new Central Union Terminal in 1950. Today the structure represents an investment of $4,856,745 and in the year 1956 land and property taxes totaling $42,745 were paid on it.

Fourteen miles from downtown is the Toledo Express Airport, served by Capital, Delta, and United. Convairs, DC-6B's and Viscounts serve the facility; non-stop flights to both New York and Chicago are available. The airport, built entirely with city funds, was completed in 1955. In 1957 its financial statement looked like this:

Gross operating revenues:	$192,660
Gross operating expense	$209,026
Operating deficit:	$ 16,366

Toledo Express Airport maintains depreciation records though such a charge is not included in operating expense. The annual depreciation charge on such items as hangars, runways and fencing is $86,851 which, if added to the deficit, brings the figure to $103,217. Moreover, there is the matter of debt service. The airport, valued at $3,865,228, was financed out of city funds and a bond issue. No interest on the amount borrowed is included in the airport statement, but at the 2-1/2 per cent rate applicable, the amount is $96,631—which boosts the deficit to $199,848.

No taxes are levied upon the publicly owned airport, of course, but if it were a private concern taxed at current rates the bill would be $45,005. This brings the 1957 deficit to $244,853.

from "Who Shot the Passenger Train?"
by David P. Morgan
TRAINS, April 1959

H. H Harwood Jr.

An NYC porter awaits his passengers in Cleveland in December 1962. The car and adjacent coach will be picked up by the eastbound *Fifth Avenue/Cleveland Limited* for delivery to Grand Central Terminal the next morning. The Pullman Company's code forbade hands in pockets.

The prototype cars had been in service on the Burlington Route since 1956 on its *Denver Zephyr*.

The new service quickly proved to be popular and while reluctant to lease more cars, NYC decided it was worthwhile to rebuild ten of the (1948) Budd-built 22-roomette *Harbor*-series cars into 16-roomette/10-bedroom sleepercoaches. The cars were returned to Budd for the rebuilding and were pressed into service on the *Wolverine, Ohio State Limited, New England States, Fifth Avenue/Cleveland Limited* and the *Chicagoan* by mid-1962. The four Budd-leased cars were then assigned to the *20th Century Limited*. When the lease ran out in 1964, these cars went to the Northern Pacific Railway and were replaced on the *20th Century Limited* with the newly rebuilt sleepercoaches.

While definitely not of first-class accommodation standards (the roomettes were quite small and the bedrooms not much larger, having been converted from Pullman-sized roomettes), they did provide privacy and a berth in which to sleep.

The Chicago-New York main line service was the standard by which the New York Central trains would be measured. The trains which ran (raced) head-to-head out of Englewood with those of the Pennsylvania were among the elite of America's passenger trains and provided the links which brought the cities along the "Water Level Route" together.

H. H Harwood jr

E7 No. 4023 leads a GP9 with Train 35, The *Iroquois* (which by 1959 originated in Albany with a Boston Beeliner connection) up the passenger ramp to the line which heads for Cleveland Union Terminal. In this October 1959 view the freight line bypass (which leads to today's Amtrak station) is at lower left. The freight line ramp to East Cleveland is at extreme left.

THE PACEMAKER

Nos. 1 and 2

The *Pacemaker* was New York Central's premier all-coach train between Chicago and New York City and was one of the first trains to receive a matching set of all new Budd equipment in 1948. In 1947, before the arrival of the new Budd cars, the train left Chicago at 3:30 in the afternoon with stops in Englewood, Gary, South Bend, Elkhart and Toledo, bypassing Cleveland Union Terminal with a service stop at Buffalo. The next scheduled stop was Harmon for a

Once a patron arrived at the gate, however, it must have become apparent that the trains were one in the same with the *Pacemaker's* cars at the rear and the *Advance Commodore Vanderbilt's* Pullmans at the front of the train, separated by a twin-unit diner set in the middle. The Los Angeles to New York 4-4-2 from the Southern Pacific/Rock Island was cut in with the 6-double bedroom/lounge, two 10-6s and a 22-roomette car. No doubt, some questions must have been asked by the *Advance Commodore's* patrons as they passed the observation car with the *Pacemaker* tail sign.

In 1955, another change occurred when the *Advance Commodore Vanderbilt* was dropped and four 10-roomette/6-double bedroom cars and two 22-roomette sleepers, a lounge car and a "thrift grill" diner were added to the consist of westbound No. 1. The observation coach was then referenced as an observation "tavern lounge coach."

Harold B. Williams, H. H. Harwood Jr. Collection

The steam powered "All-Coach" *Pacemaker* departs Englewood on Chicago's South Side in July 1949. Observation tavern lounge 48 is on the rear. The black locomotive looks strangely out of place with this 13 car train. The twin-unit diner is located roughly in the middle. Nine coaches are in the consist. To the right are the tracks of the Pennsylvania Railroad.

switch to electric power, arriving in Grand Central Terminal at 9:30 A.M.—a 17-hour run.

In 1949, the new equipment had arrived and while on essentially the same schedule, arrival in New York was at 8:50 A.M., cutting the run from 17 hours to 16 hours and 20 minutes. The train was re-equipped and put on a schedule matching that of the fastest limiteds.

The trains consisted of one of the baggage dormitory cars, coaches, a twin-unit diner (with the lounge in the kitchen portion of the set) and one of the new observation lounge "coach" buffet cars (of the 48-51-series).

In 1950, a peculiar change took place when the "all-coach" *Pacemaker* was combined with the "all-Pullman" *Advance Commodore Vanderbilt* both eastbound and westbound until 1955. The schedules were placed side by side giving the illusion that there were actually two trains. In fact, in the consist section of the timetable, the two trains are listed separately and make no mention of the other.

Eastbound No. 2, carrying a lounge car, two 10-6s, "thrift grill," coaches and observation, was combined with No. 58, the *Cleveland Limited*, at Cleveland which consisted of a 6-bedroom/lounge and four or five sleepers (a 4-4-2; a 13-double bedroom car; a 10-6; a 22-roomette; and Saturday only 10-6) on a 17- hour schedule.

The match didn't last long, however. In 1956 the *Pacemaker* was on its own schedule as the *Cleveland Limited* was combined with the *Southwestern Limited* east of Cleveland as cost trimming began. No. 2 also lost its observation car, and its westbound counterpart carried an observation car as far as Buffalo.

In 1957, No. 1 lost its observation car because it complicated switching of additional cars and was costly to operate. In 1958, westbound No. 1 was dropped from the timetable and eastbound No. 2 was combined with the *Fifth Avenue Special* at Cleveland.

In 1959, the schedule was lengthened to 19 hours. Starting in 1961, No. 2 was combined with the *New England States* from Chicago as far as Cleveland, where

While this is a posed shot, this view of the observation lounge of the *Pacemaker* is a time capsule, of sorts. These peop aren't going to church—this was how people dressed when traveling. Travel on the train (or plane) merited getting dresse up. There's not a T-shirt to be seen and considering this is a publicity photo, note that one person can be seen holding a ci; arette.

N.Y.C. Gets New Budd-built Observation Cars for "Pacemaker"

The New York Central inaugurated its new all-coach "Pacemaker" passenger service between New York and Chicago o February 11 with simultaneous eastbound and westbound runs. Receipt of two new observation cars enabled the New Yor Central to send the all-stainless steel train on its twin runs as the road's first new postwar train. All cars on the "Pacemaker were built by the Budd Company.

Each of the new "Pacemakers" consists of a 4,000-hp (sic) Diesel-electric locomotive, a baggage-dormitory car, a kitcher lounge car and an accompanying full-length dining car seating 64 persons, 56-passenger coaches and an observation car. Th new observation cars have three sections: a club section at the forward end, with seating space for 22 passengers; a loung section in the middle, accommodating 21 passengers; a rear observation section with room for 10 passengers. In the obser vation cars are such features as plexiglass partitions, fluorescent lighting combining overhead units with cove lighting alor the outside walls, radio broadcast reception, and writing desks and card tables. There are also sofas and club chairs.

(Excerpted from Railway Age - February 14, 194

the trains were separated (until April 1962, after which they split at Buffalo). At that time the *Pacemaker* carried its own 6-double bedroom/lounge car between Chicago and New York, two 10-6s, a Cleveland-to-Albany 10-6, a Cincinnati-to-Albany 10-6 (from Number 16 at Cleveland), a Pittsburgh-to-Albany 10-6 (from Pittsburgh & Lake Erie's No. 277-NYC 272 at Ashtabula, Ohio), a Pittsburgh-to-Toronto 10-6 (from the same P&LE train at Ashtabula to No. 371 at Buffalo), and an Indianapolis to New York 10-6 (from No. 312-the *Southwestern Limited* at Cleveland), reclining seat coaches from Chicago to New York and from Pittsburgh to Buffalo, in addition to a parlor buffet lounge car from Buffalo.

In October 1961, sleeper service was cut back to provide a Chicago-New York 10-6 and Cincinnati-New York 10-6 from the *Ohio State Limited* at Buffalo.

In April 1962, the Cincinnati connection was eliminated with only the single Chicago-New York 10-6 remaining, along with the 6-double bedroom/lounge, coaches and diner. With the October 1963 timetable, the 10-6 was gone and No. 2 became coach-only with No. 28's dining/lounge cars serving No. 2's coach passengers.

Coincident with the 1964 World's Fair in New York, No. 2 listed coaches in addition to a Cleveland-New York (except Saturday) 6-bedroom/lounge, serving "sandwiches and beverages" and breakfast buffet, and a Sunday-only parlor buffet lounge, Buffalo-New York.

By April 1966, No. 2 originated in Buffalo for the run to Grand Central Terminal. Departing at 5:25 A.M., it carried a 6-bedroom/lounge from the *Ohio State Limited* and coaches. By October 1966, the *Pacemaker* was removed from the timetable altogether.

Steam was still pulling the trains of the Great Steel Fleet when this shot of the *Pacemaker* at Oscawana, New York was made on July 12, 1952. The all-Budd appearance has been altered by the inclusion of a Pullman-Standard baggage dormitory car. The Niagara, NYC's most powerful steam locomotive, would soon be confined to the Big Four route.

J. R. Quinn Collection

THE CLEVELAND LIMITED

Nos. 57 and 58

The *Cleveland Limited* was one of New York Central's crack limiteds running between Cleveland and New York. In 1947, the *Cleveland Limited* was an all-Pullman train carrying a mix of heavyweight "standard" cars and new streamline equipment, including a diner from Albany. Its westbound counterpart carried a single coach between Grand Central Terminal and Albany. It left Cleveland Union Terminal at 8:30 P.M. for arrival at Grand Central at 8:00 A.M. the next morning.

In 1949, the train carried the newly-acquired equipment from Budd and Pullman-Standard and listed a 4-compartment/4-double bedroom/2-drawing room car (4-4-2) from the early 1940s. Its schedule was advanced somewhat to an 8:00 P.M. departure with an early 7:15 A.M. arrival in New York City.

While carrying only streamline sleeping cars between Cleveland and New York eastbound, its counterpart No. 57 carried a mix of standard and streamline equipment for Cincinnati (a 12-section/1-drawing room Pullman), a Boston to Cincinnati 8-section/1-drawing room/2-compartment Pullman, a Boston to Cleveland 10-6 and a Toronto to Cleveland 12-section/1-drawing room car from Buffalo, in addition to that lonely coach to Albany. This was standard practice until 1953 when the Toronto and Boston cars were redeployed.

In 1953, Nos. 57 and 58 carried a 6-bedroom/lounge (serving a breakfast buffet), a 4-4-2, a 13-bedroom car, a 10-6 and two 22-roomette cars.

By 1955, while still listing only sleeping cars, No. 58 was combined with No. 2, the *Pacemaker*, for the run to New York and westbound, combined with No. 59, the *Chicagoan*, with no change in accommodations.

In October 1956, some more rearranging commenced as No. 59 left Cleveland at 9:00 P.M. for a 7:55 A.M. arrival at Grand Central Terminal, and westbound leaving Grand Central at 8:15 P.M. for a 7:50 A.M. arrival in Cleveland Union Terminal. Having a compliment of sleepers for Toronto and Buffalo, it lost its all-Pullman status with the addition of coaches.

The next major change came in October 1958 when, in another realignment, the eastbound No. 58 was combined with No. 6, the *Fifth Avenue Special* from Chicago, becoming No. 6 the *Fifth Avenue-Cleveland Limited*. No. 57 remained, leaving New York at 7:30 P.M. but terminating at Toledo at 10:20 A.M. the next morning. Beginning in 1960, it terminated at Cleveland at 8:00 A.M.

The new No. 6 picked up cars for New York originating at Toledo (a 10-6); at Cleveland: a 10-6, a 13-double bedroom Pullman, two 22-roomette cars, and two 10-6s from St. Louis; at Syracuse: a 10-6 and a 10-5 (Saturday only) from Massena. The St. Louis cars were from No. 312, the *Southwestern Limited*, including a 6-double bedroom/lounge and coaches as service to St. Louis was rapidly evaporating.

In 1962, No. 6 picked up a 10-6 sleeper from Lake Placid at Utica and 10-6s, one each, from Detroit, Buffalo, Rochester and Syracuse and carried one of the rebuilt 22-roomette sleepercoaches, Cleveland to New York City.

In 1966, No. 57 became a New York to Chicago almost-all-stops run offering sleeping car service New York to Cleveland, a 6-double bedroom/lounge, and a 10-6; a 10-6 to Toronto; coaches New York to Cleveland, and coaches daily Cleveland to Chicago.

The schedules for Nos. 6 and 57 remained fairly constant, but in October 1967, the westbound No. 57 lost its name and became a nondescript number carrying coaches and a buffet/lounge New York to Buffalo, while No. 6 still carried a vestige of its former self, a 10-6 from Cleveland, a sleepercoach, diner and coaches.

Train No. 6, the *Fifth Avenue Cleveland Limited* is carrying two unusual Santa Fe baggage cars equipped with six wheel trucks at Toledo on August 15, 1965. The tracks to adjacent platforms on the left have already been removed

Louis A. Marre Collection

THE COMMODORE VANDERBILT

Nos. 67 and 68

Second only to the *20th Century Limited* in status and equipment, the *Commodore Vanderbilt* was an all-Pullman train in 1948 carrying the *20th Century Limited's* hand-me-downs in addition to new Pullman-Standard equipment. Nos. 67 & 68 provided a 6-double bedroom/lounge-buffet of the *Lake* series, twin-unit diner/lounge (and, on occasion, a twin-unit set with stainless steel fluted sides under the window band from the canceled Chesapeake and Ohio order), 4-4-2s, 10-6s, 13-double bedroom cars and 22-roomette cars in addition to one of the four former 1938 *20th Century Limited* observation cars of the *Island*-series.

In 1949, No. 68 left Chicago at 3:00 P.M. for an 8:20 A.M. arrival in New York. Grand Central Terminal departures were at 3:45 P.M. for a 7:40 A.M. arrival at La Salle Street. Through the years, the *Commodore's* departure times and arrivals varied slightly and included only a couple of more stops than the *20th Century Limited*— Elkhart and Toledo. In all other respects, a trip on the *Commodore Vanderbilt* was just as elegant and prestigious as on the *20th Century Limited*, if one didn't need a haircut en route or the services of the train's stenographer.

While NYC provided connecting transcontinental service with the Burlington, Union Pacific (via Chicago & North Western and Milwaukee Road) and Santa Fe, the transcontinental cars (up to 1953 from Los Angeles over the Union Pacific/Chicago and North Western) were carried on No. 65, the *Advance Commodore Vanderbilt*, but,

W. G. Fancher, H. H. Harwood Jr. Collection

The "Pullman Car only" *Commodore Vanderbilt* quickly departs Englewood with four double bedroom Thousand Islands, one of the four observation cars of the 1938 20th Century Limited (now assigned to Nos. 67 and 68) on the rear. The Pullman name is still on the car in this picture, made in 1949. Up ahead are two 10-6s, two 12-double bedroom cars, four 22-roomette cars, twin unit lounge diner, 6 double-bedroom lounge car and baggage dormitory car.

Slump Benches NYC Commodore

Badly slumped first-class patronage has forced the New York Central to take off its "Commodore Vanderbilt" until after Labor Day.

The train's coaches will be added to the hitherto all-Pullman "Twentieth Century" which is to run at standard fares and with less frill-services than normally are offered on it.

A spokesman for that road said that what is being done is to consolidate the two New York-Chicago trains, running them both on the current "Century" schedules.

The Central's hostesses will continue to grace the road's most luxurious equipment but the barber and valet services will be curtailed.

The Central officer said the move is not an extraordinary one and had been contemplated before. Slumping summer Pullman travel on the Central had seen the "Commodore" travel as light as 68-70 passengers, he said, a condition that made it hard to make the train pay. He assured a reporter, however, that this was not a precursor to an eventual elimination of the train year-round.

He insisted further that the recent 15% first-class fare rise on the New York Central was not a contributory factor to the traffic decline.

Actually, he said, there had been a last-minute rush to buy tickets just before the fares went up (the advance sale comes to about $750,000 for the system, a third of this at New York City) and the road expects that it will be several months before the effect of the fare boost can be evaluated.

(Excerpted from Railway Age, August 5, 1957)

effective December 6, 1953, the eastbound cars off the UP/CNW were carried on No. 67. This was a streamline 10-6 and it was common to see the bright yellow cars of the Union Pacific Railroad in New York City being switched at Mott Haven yard. On Saturday-only in 1956, the *Commodore Vanderbilt* carried the *Super Chief* car to and from Chicago and in July, lost its *Island* observation cars just for the summer when the train was combined with the *Pacemaker*.

In October 1956, the *Commodore Vanderbilt* carried a car each for the *City of San Francisco* and the *California Zephyr* (both 10-6s) and began carrying coaches, the end of its all-Pullman status, although the refurbished 4-double bedroom *Island* observation cars were reinstated.

Effective April 27, 1958, however, the *Commodore's* coaches were added to the *20th Century Limited* running as a "combined" train (and from the perspective of the timetable, either the *20th Century Limited* gained coaches or the *Commodore Vanderbilt* lost its Pullmans and finally lost its identity with the publication of the October 30, 1960 timetable. The *Commodore Vanderbilt* one of the proudest names in the Great Steel Fleet, was sacrificial victim of the times.

H.H. Harwood

A T-3 electric motor takes the combined *Advance Commodore Vanderbilt* and *Pacemaker* through Spuyten Duyvil toward Harmon in May 1954. Behind the T-motor is the *Advance Commodore's* baggage/dormitory. The forward portion of the train is No. 65.

THE 20TH CENTURY LIMITED
Nos. 25 and 26

The *20th Century Limited* was the flagship of the New York Central System to which all other trains were subordinate. A voyage on the *20th Century Limited* began with the patron traversing the famous 260 foot red carpet. Train staff wore smart and dignified uniforms and were attentive to every detail of comfort. Traveling the *20th Century Limited* added a new dimension to the term "first- class." It was, without doubt, "the greatest train in the world," and was known for transporting the distinguished, the rich, and the famous.

Continuing a tradition established in 1902, the *20th Century Limited* received a full complement of Pullman-Standard-built cars in 1948 in the new two-tone gray color scheme of 1946, with distinctive "lookout lounge" observation cars adorned with the regal light blue drumhead to mark the train's passing (the others on the system were red). The train's lounge cars, *Atlantic Shore* and *Lake Shore* along with its dining car sets were also specifically built for *20th Century Limited* service.

Although it is uncertain how it was intended, a select few of the 1948 cars from Pullman were equipped with a special electro-pneumatic braking system exclusively for use on the *20th Century Limited*. Thirteen of the 10-6 *River*-series cars and 12 of the 12-double bedroom *Port*-series were initially designated for *20th Century Limited* service with the new braking system.

It is unlikely that the system was ever used, for in order for the system to work, all the cars in the train would had to have been equipped in the same fashion. The dining cars, *Lake* and *Atlantic Shore* cars and the two *Creek* observation cars did not have this system. It can be surmised that during the course of the construction of the large order, the railroad changed its mind and the cars were then retrofitted with the standard Westinghouse air brake system.

Furthermore, the locomotives from EMD, normally the assigned power for the *20th Century Limited*, would also have to be equipped in order to make use of such a system, which they were not. There is also a feeling that within the mechanical and operating departments, that there might be some resistance to electricians working on air brake systems. Such are the ways of any organization.

Interspersed with the 22-roomette cars, the 12-double bedroom cars and the ubiquitous 10-6s were some of the newly refurbished 4-4-2s of the 1940s and the new spacious mid-train lounge offering a barbershop, stenographer/train secretary and a shower, one of two twin-unit diners (and kitchen dormitory for the crew) and one of the 1938 mail/baggage cars. The train also carried a transcontinental sleeper from the Santa Fe (either up front directly behind the mail/baggage car or directly in front of the observation) and for a brief period even sported a couple of its own 4-4-2 Pullman cars with silver trucks, ostensibly for the transcontinental service with the Santa Fe's *Chief* and *Super Chief*, a service which ended in February 1958.

The train was extra fare, all-Pullman, leaving New York at 6:00 P.M. for an 8:45 A.M. arrival in Chicago; 4:45 P.M. from Chicago to New York arriving at 9:30 A.M. (in 1957). Here, like the *New England States*, departures didn't change much and stops were limited—only at Englewood and Harmon. Train staff wore special uniforms with a *20th Century Limited* patch on the left arm and, beginning in 1956, both trains employed a stewardess, called a "Century Girl," to assist passengers en route.

In the summer of 1957, the *20th Century Limited* carried coaches (during the *Commodore's* hiatus) for the first time—just for the summer—but it was an omen.

With the April 1958 timetable, the *20th Century Limited* again lost its all-Pullman extra fare status with the addition of coaches, albeit temporarily, and its schedule was expanded to include Gary, South Bend, Elkhart, and Toledo. The *Lake* and *Atlantic Shore* cars were removed, later being sold to the Rock Island; the *20th Century Limited's* twin-unit diner/kitchen/dormitory sets were briefly reassigned to the *Wolverine* and on occasion the *Iroquois*, while the *Commodore's* twin-unit diner/kitchen/ lounge set was substituted; a tavern/lounge car was added for the coach section and a

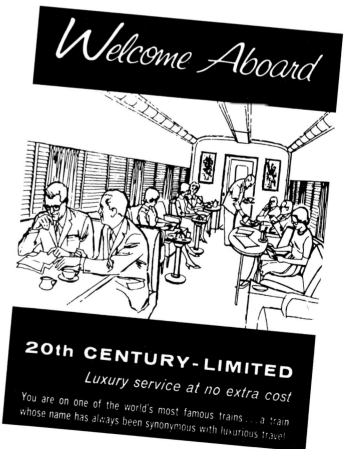

Welcome Aboard

20th CENTURY-LIMITED
Luxury service at no extra cost
You are on one of the world's most famous trains... a train whose name has always been synonymous with luxurious travel!

baggage/dormitory added for the dining car staff. Technically, the *20th Century Limited* was "combined" with the *Commodore Vanderbilt* which had obtained coaches beginning in October 1956. In fact, the *Commodore's* identical schedule was printed alongside the *20th Century Limited's* to give the appearance of a separate train. Perhaps the traffic department wasn't emotionally ready to publicly drop the train or admit to a downgrading in its passenger service.

In October 1959, the *Century* briefly regained its all-Pullman status, losing the coaches and gaining one of the new 24-8 Budd-built sleepercoaches. At this point in time reference to the *Commodore Vanderbilt* ceased. Six months later, in April 1960, the coaches were back. The *Creek* observation cars were technically the only cars left

in the consist from the original 1948 Pullman order which had been specifically built and assigned for *20th Century Limited* service.

In 1960, the *20th Century Limited* still listed an impressive consist: a baggage/mail car, baggage dormitory, stainless steel Budd coaches (usually only a couple or just one), a Budd grill diner, a sleepercoach, the two-tone gray diner set, a 22-roomette, three 10-6s, four 12-double bedroom cars and one of the *Creek* observation cars. The forward portion of the *20th Century Limited* was all Budd stainless steel, with the exception of the head end cars.

In 1962, the *20th Century Limited* celebrated its 60th anniversary. A number of cars were refurbished and the "*Century*" name was added to each car assigned to *Century* service, usually located by the vestibule doors. On the Budd-built cars, a plate was affixed by the door with the name, "*Century*."

Passengers received complimentary boutonnieres (for the men) and corsages (for the ladies), freshly cut flowers appeared in the diners and observation cars, and while these were small amenities they were an attempt to restore some of the lost elegance.

NYC Photo, J. W. Swanberg Collection

This oft-reproduced press run photo of the *20th Century Limited* at Breakneck Mountain is notable because it shows the first sleeper (*Imperial House*) after the baggage/RPO car with silver trucks. The 4-4-2 was used in transcontinental service with the Santa Fe.

Philip Doughty

In 1964, the lease ran out on the four 24-8 sleeper-coaches which had been in service since 1959. Two of the 1962 Budd rebuilt sleepercoaches were then substituted on each train and remained in service until the end in December 1967.

Toward the end, as the gray 1948 Pullman-Standard cars aged and were sold to other railroads and overall sleeping car service demand lessened, stainless steel Budd equipment was substituted for the elegant gray Pullman cars and it was not uncommon to see the *20th Century Limited* with the gray twin-unit diner, one or a couple of the 12-double bedroom cars and either of the *Creek*-series cars or the Budd-built *Wingate Brook* (built for the *Southwestern Limited* in 1948) bringing up the rear. In fact, in late 1967, so few of the gray Pullmans were left that it was possible to see an all stainless steel *20th Century Limited*.

By 1967, only three of the gray Pullman-Standard 10-6s remained in service; all the gray 22-roomette cars had been sold by 1962 (and most of them in 1959); twelve of the fourteen 12-double bedroom cars lasted until 1968. The twin-unit diners from the *Commodore* lasted in service until 1971 when they were scrapped.

On November 5, 1967 the *20th Century Limited* and the *New England States* were combined west of Buffalo in a further attempt to curtail losses. Meanwhile, passenger trains across the nation were rapidly becoming victims of the times and no amount of cost cutting could make the trains break even, let alone restore profits. What had begun fifteen years earlier as the public's slow defection had become by the late 1960s a wholesale abandonment of rail passenger travel.

In a period of three years, abetted by the loss of the mail contracts, the rate of passenger losses literally accelerated to the point of no return. Then, on an appropriately dreary December 2, 1967 with little publicity, the *Centuries* made their final departures from New York and Chicago—and the Great Steel Fleet passed into history.

Philip Dough

As the sun breaks through the clouds the 20th Century Limited, which moments before clattered through the diamond crossing the Monon Railroad at Otis, Indiana, rounds the curve at MP 472 in May 1959.

Twentieth Century Limited of November 8-9, 1966 at Grand Central Terminal

Number	Type		On November 9, 1966, the *Century* consisted of	
			Number	Type
236	P-2b electric locomotive		235	P-2b electric locomotive
5018	RPO		5017	RPO
8979	Budd baggage/dormitory car		8977	Budd baggage/dormitory
2926	Budd coach		2908	Budd coach
462	Budd grill diner		455	Budd grill diner
10815	Sleepercoach		10817	Sleepercoach
479-404	Budd twin-unit diner		10813	Sleepercoach
Orchard Valley	Budd sleeper		476-402	Pullman twin-unit diner
Putnam Valley	Budd sleeper		*Champlain Valley*	Budd sleeper
Port of Chicago	Pullman		*Peaceful Valley*	Budd sleeper
Hickory Creek	Pullman Observation.		*Port of Detroit*	Pullman
			Wingate Brook	Budd Observation

The *Wingate Brook* was similar in floor plan to the *Creek* cars, the regular two *Century* observation cars, and was kept at Chicago and used only when one of the *Creek* cars was out of service.

J. W. Swanberg

"The Mystery of the *Century*"

Railfans who have watched the classic (1959) Alfred Hitchcock film, *North by Northwest* always watch carefully for the scenes which ere shot at Grand Central Terminal and aboard the *20th Century Limited*. During the segment, Cary Grant boards the *20th Century* at CT and walks by a NYC gray car lettered *Imperial State*, which was one of nine 4-4-2 sleeping cars built by Pullman-Standard in 1939.

What is interesting about this car is that in the upper corner of the car there is a "marker light" which seems to indicate that the r is not the real *Imperial State*. The car actually appears to be one of a type which was purchased by the Southern Pacific Railway and sed as the tail car on the *City of San Francisco* and the *Cascade*. The car is actually what is called a "blunt-end" 10-6 and was a rarity.

So, why did Hitchcock use this car at Grand Central Terminal? The answer seems to lie in the fact that the shot was actually *remade* Hollywood.

If one watches closely when Cary Grant emerges in a Red Cap's uniform at La Salle Street Station, he passes the real *Imperial State* nd a 22-roomette *Quincy Bay* and then two very quiet E8s.

Something went wrong with the shooting in Grand Central and in order to recreate and insure "continuity," a term used by oviemakers to insure that the same objects from one scene appear in different "takes" of the same scene, he needed and obtained a eeping car. The Southern Pacific supplied the car and painted it to look like the NYC *Imperial State*.

The scenes which appear to be taken at Grand Central Terminal were actually shot on location. The film crew also filmed shots of e *20th Century* at twilight along the Hudson River, but the interior shots were made in a studio, with the exception of the dining car cenes which were shot aboard an NYC twin-unit diner, but probably not on the *20th Century Limited*. It looks real, though.

In Chicago, two E8s were coupled to a string of NYC gray cars, including the aforementioned *Imperial State* and *Quincy Bay*. loticeably absent, of course, is the ever-present RPO.

Hitchcock was a master of detail. The scene with the *Imperial State* appears to be shot at Grand Central Terminal, but actually the ntire scene was shot on a recreated setting which was made to look like the Grand Central Terminal platform. Things are not always hat they appear to be in the movies!

J. W. Swanberg

ectric T-3a 282 is at Irvington, New York on December 30, 1960 leading the eastbound *20th Century Limited*. Behind the elec-ic is one of the RPO cars built for the 1938 version of the same train. A Pullman-Standard baggage/dormitory is next. The tter normally accommodated the dining car staff.

The *20th Century Limited* has arrived, its passengers have disembarked and the train's staff packs up and leaves the train in the hands of the car cleaners. Here the train secretary, dictaphone in his right hand walks through the empty lounge of one of the Shore cars.

NYC Photo, Theodore Shrady Collection

Telephone service was available aboard the *Shore* cars when they ran in the 20th Century Limited. A train secretary was also available for important business matters.

NYC Photo, J. W. Swanberg Collection

T. J. Donahue

The westbound *20th Century Limited* is at Breakneck Mountain in August 1963 led by three forlorn looking E7s heading into the sunset. Notice that the middle unit has a different stripe scheme (it doesn't have the zig zag) at the end of the carbody similar to the freight locomotives. This may have been an experimental scheme or perhaps a mistake at the paint shop.

Leo Witucki, Victor A. Baird Collection

A gleaming *20th Century Limited* passes over the track pans at Lydick, Indiana on a clear summer morning in 1953. It's hard o believe that the train was moving at 80 mph when it was frozen in time—over forty years ago.

FOND MEMORIES

In June 1961, when I was eleven years old, my mother died and two weeks later, my grandfather followed her. My father had my mother transported east from Chicago aboard the *New England States* as far as Pittsfield, Massachusetts.

He decided we should spend the Christmas Holiday with my grandmother in Williamstown, Massachusetts, where both my mother and grandfather were laid to rest. Dad booked himself, me and my older brother aboard the *New England States*, a train we had taken east every summer.

It was quite an adventure. My brother had "dibs" on the roomette, so I got the upper berth in the bedroom which I shared with my father. On the return trip we would ride in one of the new sleepercoaches.

My brother and I were captivated with a new Revere tape recorder our father had purchased and we decided to take it along with us. It was big and heavy and I wound up carrying it because I was the one who was really keen on the idea of bringing it.

It was cold in Chicago on the day of our departure and after parking the car in a parking garage (my Dad gave the attendant a ten dollar bill to "look after it"), I carried that Revere the two blocks to La Salle Street Station. After battling the wind and cold for the first couple of minutes, I had second thoughts about this project. Soon

we were walking through the doors of the station and it felt like reaching the Promised Land! Before long, I thought, we'd be on the train!

Waiting to board the train was an experience mixed with anticipation and frustration—like waiting those last few minutes to open the presents at Christmas. I was anxious and I couldn't wait for the gatekeeper to open the heavy iron sliding door. I could see the train on the other side and I wanted to be on it. When the door finally did open, the three of us set forth on our expedition.

Our gray Pullman was way up front. Steam hissed from between the cars. A sense of excitement filled the air. The train was a mix of 18 Pullman and Budd cars and had three locomotive units and two diners, one of which was of the twin-unit variety. My brother said to me, "Let's stick the microphone out the window (Dutch door) and make a recording of the train sounds!" Great idea!

We had brought along an extension cord and while Dad was getting settled, we set up the recorder in the vestibule, laying the power cord down the aisle to a nearby 110 volt outlet. As the porter lifted the step box from the platform and into the car, my brother asked him if he could give us an "all aboard," just for effect.

He gleefully consented and looked at us for a moment as we heard the train's conductor several cars back intone a, "BOARRRRD!" a la a Metropolitan Opera tenor. My brother cued the porter. He closed the trap with a loud "*CLAP!*" then, "AAALL ABOARD." "*BANG!*" went the bot-

The *New England States* passes by the Chicago, South Shore & South Bend Railroad upon its approach to the Art Deco Sout Bend station. Train No. 28 is led by an A-B formation of E7s in this summer of 1953 photo. Before long, gray Pullman-Standar cars will invade the consist, but on this day the *"States"* is a sleek silver streamliner.

tom half of the door. Again, "AAALL ABOARD. Next stop will be Englewood; 63rd Street. Heh, heh."

Without as much as a nudge, the train quietly began to pull out. Within a minute we were out of the station and moving through the crossovers.

We recorded for 10 minutes before my father, noting our prolonged absence, began a search for his wayward sons—tracing the extension cord to the vestibule. And that was the end of that!

So we moved to Bedroom "E" where my brother took control holding the microphone over the open toilet to get the track sounds as we rolled by the steel mills of Gary, Indiana.

In the summer of 1969, I would be traveling aboard Penn Central's Train No. 28 for a trip to Pittsfield, as I had on so many occasions before. Being an economy-minded college student, I booked a roomette in the Boston section's sleepercoach. By then, La Salle Street departures had been moved to Union Station which was being systematically demolished, and Penn Central was proving to be less than a smooth operation.

I was delighted to find that the last car was an ex-New Haven 14-4 (*Sandy Point*), even if it was lettered for its new owner and sported a green window band stripe replacing the New Haven's familiar orange. What I hadn't expected was that SC28, the sleepercoach, was a (still painted) tuscan red Pennsy 10-6, *Catawissa Rapids*, a product of Pullman. My sleepercoach was a "Pullman" and all for the price of a sleepercoach! What a deal. How the two people (who were paying full first-class fares for their similar accommodations) in the New Haven Pullman felt, I could only surmise.

The porter cheerfully greeted me and confirmed my quizzical expressions about the "sleepercoach." Penn Central, it seemed, was having some equipment problems. He took me to my roomette and said he'd be back.

Did I need anything? We'd be leaving shortly.

He excused himself and a few minutes later I heard him play a small glockenspiel, starting at the vestibule, working his way back to the rear of the car, intoning, "AAAll visitors off, please. The train leaves in five minutes. AAAll visitors off." The way he said, "AAAll," had a familiar ring to it.

I followed him to the end of the car where he continued this standard Pullman tradition, probably one of the last porters to do so, I figured. I followed in his wake and ducked into an open bedroom as he passed by in the opposite direction.

"First stop will be Englewood; 63rd Street." Could it be? When he stopped, I asked if he recalled one Christmas many years ago when two boys brought a tape recorder on board the *New England States* to record train sounds. Was he an ex-NYC porter? "No," he replied. He was an ex-*Pullman* porter, but he worked on the NYC and he did remember! We shared a great laugh at this chance encounter.

The next day, I stepped off the train - a baggage car and a diner (added at Albany), a coach and the two sleepers—at the "new" Pittsfield station. We shook hands, and as I slipped him a five dollar bill, I repeated how nice it was to reminisce with him.

I happily greeted my Uncle Bob who came to meet me and told him that I wanted to wait to see the train leave. As the last two cars drifted past the parking lot on that bright sunny August morn, I spied the porter standing in the vestibule doorway. When he spotted me, we simultaneously raised our hands and waved to each other.

"Who's that?" my uncle asked. "Someone you know?"

"Yeah," I replied. "An old friend."

G.H.D.

Philip Doughty

Train No. 28, The *New England States*, glides out of Albany Union Station. The train carries holiday travelers and extra sleepers in this December 23, 1962 scene. Behind the baggage dormitory are the warm and inviting Budd buffet lounge and one of the 7 Pullman-Standard diners. This view was taken from the *Trinity River* as it crossed the Hudson River.

Leo Witucki, Victor Baird Collectio.

The *Aerotrain* passes through Niles, Michigan on a bright summer day in 1956. The design features were straight off of the GM drawing boards, not unlike the Chevrolet being advertised in the foreground. Did GM ever consider building an *Aeroplane* Many of the car design features mimic the airplane interiors not unlike todays Amfleet cars.

The *Xplorer* is entering Cincinnati Union Terminal in May 1956. The Baldwin locomotive was powered by a 1000 HP V-12 Maybach diesel rated at 570 HP for heating, A/C and lighting. The 4 speed hydraulic transmission was the source of much of its problems.

Leo Witucki, Victor Baird Collectic

Train No. 35, the *Iroquois* is leaving South Bend, Indiana with three units and a considerable amount of head end business in his May 18, 1962 scene.

The westbound *James Whitcomb Riley* has arrived at Indianapolis Union Station in March 1956. Today the trainshed is used as a food court as well as for Amtrak (the tracks on the left) in a revitalized Union Station which also houses a Holiday Inn!

The train information board showing departures indicates a combined *Commodore Vanderbilt* and *20th Century Limited* November 1959.

Twilight in The Berkshires

The <u>new</u> *New England States* —

now complete from Diesel to Observation Lounge!

It's an all-private-room Dreamliner . . . with rubber-foam mattresses

and circulating ice water in every room . . . an enclosed lavatory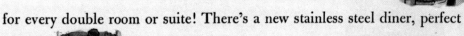

for every double room or suite! There's a new stainless steel diner, perfect

setting for the royal meals and hospitality of the New England States.

And there's a luxurious observation car for refreshments and relaxation . . .

Eastbound or Westbound you sleep on the smooth Water Level Route

and see the picturesque Berkshires by day . . . on your way between the

Heart of Chicago and the Hub  of New England.

The Water Level Route —You Can Sleep

NEW YORK CENTRAL
BOSTON & ALBANY ROUTE

On January 31, 1963 the crew of Train No. 59, The *Chicagoan* receives orders at South Bend, Indiana for the last leg westwar to Chicago.

NEW *Streamliners and Dreamliners...*

Headliners in New York Central's
1947 Luxury Parade!

This is your Travel Year

Miles of new, streamlined coaches are here. And close on their wheels will follow more miles of all-private-room sleeping cars for a new fleet of overnight *Dreamliners*. All part of the $100,000,000 program now spotlighting the *new* in New York Central!

New Days of Delight

Sink back into the depths of a reclining seat aboard one of New York Central's post-war coaches. Enjoy the year round comfort of clean, conditioned air. Watch America roll past your wide-view window at scenic level. Dine in thrifty new coffee-shop cars. Lounge in luxurious new coach observation cars. In short, *fare like a king at low coach fares!*

New Dream Trips by Night

Relax in the privacy of your own completely equipped room. Or enjoy the sociability of Central's smart new club cars. Feast in new dining cars ... some so spacious they need separate kitchen cars. Later, sleep in a feather-soft bed as your *Dreamliner* speeds in any weather over the smooth *Water Level Route*...And arrive refreshed for the day ahead.

© 1947, New York Central Railroad Company

NEW NEW YORK CENTRAL
The Water Level Route—You Can Sleep

Louis A. Marr

No. 4058 heads up an *Ohio State Limited* at Cincinnati Union Terminal in August of 1956, while Southern units back down to their train.

Richard Cook, Sr.

rain No. 30, *The Twilight Limited* pauses at Jackson, Michigan on July 16, 1957. Just ahead of the parlor observation and coach one of the Budd twin-unit diner sets with lounge in the kitchen car. The nameboards have not yet been painted gray with luminum gray lettering. In 1958, most stainless steel cars would receive this treatment.

Geoffrey H. Dough

The glory days of the Great Steel Fleet are memories at a desolate Buffalo Central Terminal on July 8, 1987. The abandon
terminal hoisted but one visitor this day.

EPILOGUE

"In Search of the Great Steel Fleet"

Of course, New York Central's passenger operations didn't end with the final departures of the *20th Century Limited* and *New England States* on December 2, 1967. The next day, the Century's observation cars were placed in storage, all but one of the trains lost their names and were rescheduled in a format which would be copied by Penn Central in February 1968. The combined New York-Boston-Chicago train replication would eventually reappear in the form of Amtrak's *Lake Shore Limited*.

On December 3, 1967, NYC initiated its "Empire Service" between New York and Buffalo and put forward a serious effort to schedule frequent and reliable service. These trains were also replicated by Penn Central and Amtrak. No doubt however hard the effort may have been, the trains were overshadowed by their forerunners.

Never again will society witness another passenger car delivery to a private railroad equaling that made by Pullman-Standard, Budd and ACF beginning in 1948 to New York Central. NYC orders, mixed with those of the nation's other railroads, were a reflection of their confidence that the nation's transportation future would remain fixed in time; they would surpass other modes of travel and would prevail.

Time would prove otherwise. Along with the passenger train's demise went the culture of train travel, the infrastructure used to support passenger traffic, i.e. the stations, the terminals and the services of Parmelee and Traveler's Aid. Gone were the aura, mystique, and adventure of overnight and daytime travel—for many it became a nightmare as services and maintenance were reduced.

So, what happened to the fleet of cars and where did they go?

Some of the cars of the 1948 Great Steel Fleet were passed on to Penn Central. Those which weren't sold felt the scrapper's torch. Out of all the gray Pullman cars ordered in 1945, only the two twin-unit dining car sets built for the *Commodore Vanderbilt* survived into Penn Central, until they too were scrapped in 1971, clad in a pea-green color scheme.

Thirteen of the eighteen Budd grill diners and five of the twelve 44-seat diners, fifty-five of the sixty coaches, eleven of the forty 10-6s, ten of the eleven 6-double bedroom/lounge cars, and seven of the remaining ten sleepercoaches were passed on to Penn Central. Most of these were then passed on to Amtrak ownership in 1973. (Amtrak leased the Penn Central cars until that time.)

And what of the other cars? (for a more complete listing see appendix on page 109) Most went to Mexico and Canadian railroads. Of all the forty-five gray Pullman 22-roomette cars, none survived the sale to other railroads without being altered into baggage, diners or baggage/roomette cars. Not one.

The ninety-seven gray 10-6s fared better. Twenty were sold to the Canadian National; sixty-nine went to Mexico; the rest were scrapped.

Of the sixteen gray 6-double bedroom/lounges, eight survived in the hands of private owners.

All but one of the seven gray 44-seat diners were scrapped. The lone survivor went to the Delaware and Hudson Railway before being sold to the Cooperstown and Charlotte Valley Railroad, a short line in Central New York where it ran in "dinner train" service in the early 1970s.

Only the *Atlantic Shore* survived the Rock Island sale in 1958 and is in private hands.

Both gray *Creek* cars are in private custody. The *Hickory Creek* is being restored and the *Sandy Creek* has been remodeled, without bedroom facilities, for private train service.

Eleven of the fourteen 12-double bedroom cars survived the scrapper's torch. Five of the all-bedroom cars and three of the nine gray baggage/dorm cars were sold to Ringling Brothers Barnum and Bailey Circus for members of the circus family.

The single NYC Pullman stainless steel sheathed observation car built for the *Royal Palm* had a short life, being wrecked on the Union Pacific in 1951. Delivered in March 1950 for pool service out of Cincinnati for the Florida trade, lettered for NYC, it briefly graced the rear end of NYC's *Royal Palm* connection out of Detroit and held the distinction of being the only stainless steel sheathed sleeping car built for NYC by Pullman-Standard.

Of the 153 stainless steel sheathed Pullman-Standard coaches, 14 went to the Long Island Railroad, the rest to Penn Central of which 77 went briefly to Amtrak before they were scrapped or sold to short lines or private parties.

The Budd cars lasted longer because of their shot-weld all stainless steel construction. Fifteen of the forty 10-6s, along with twenty-one of the thirty-one 22-roomette sleepers went south to Mexico. All but two of the thirteen buffet/lounge cars were sold to the New Jersey Department of Transportation (NJDOT).

Three of the four *Brook* cars built for the *Ohio State Limited* and the *New England States* went to Canada before returning to the United States 20 years later. A fourth car was sold to a private party. All three of the lookout lounge *Brook*-series cars survived, one going to Canada (Algoma Central); the others are in private hands in the United States.

The four observation-buffet-lounge cars built for the *James Whitcomb Riley* and the *Pacemaker* were sold to the Kansas City Southern after being retired from main line service. They were subsequently sold to private parties.

Of the 13 observation/lounge cars, two went to Amtrak, one to a club in Iowa and the rest to NdeM.

The nine twin-unit diners built for the *Pacemaker*, *Ohio State Limited*, *New England States* and the *Southwestern Limited* were sold to Canadian roads before being scrapped only one set survived.

Likewise, of the 12 baggage/dormitory cars one was retired for work train service while the others were scrapped.

Of all the remaining Budd-built cars passed on to Amtrak by Penn Central, only the six rebuilt sleeper-coaches and only eight of the grill diners remained in service in 1995, the other Budd cars having been either sold or scrapped even these are on borrowed time.

*****

One may search for the cars and find them or visit some of the few remaining Gothic, Romanesque, or Art Deco terminals associated with the golden age of railroading. One will search in vain, however, for what was *really* lost the night the *Centuries* made their final departures - the civility of travel. Society lost so much more than passenger trains.

As the public seeks to restore train service, it has visions of better times when as a nation we were less inclined to settle for mediocrity; when "on time" meant in the station and not within ten minutes of its scheduled arrival; when travel with all of its inherent uncertainties and inconveniences was clean and comfortable, reliable and safe, an adventure without the risks, elegant and sophisticated, affordable, relaxing, and most of all, enjoyable.

Train travel could be all of these, but the trains are more memorable because of the people one would meet (trains are great for meeting people) over a freshly-cooked meal which equaled that of a fine restaurant; the associations with the travel experience which are the bridges to our past, our youth, our growing up—a rite of passage—our first trip alone; a summer vacation, a trip to a camp, a trip to visit relatives, to a wedding or a funeral. Trains took us past the borders of our worlds and transported us to worlds beyond.

Even though we enjoyed and loved the trains, they were nothing but sheets of steel without people. Beginning with a friendly wave from an unfamilier engineer, we watched and counted the cars as the streamliners sped by racing against time to the big cities; and waved again at the people gazing out of the observation car windows, lamenting that we weren't in their place.

In fact, it was the dedicated men and women of the New York Central Railroad who sought to provide a service without rival and in so doing created a standard and legacy which would last for generations. It was they who made those sheets of steel spring to life; it was they who transformed a trip into an experience.

Perhaps it is one of the enigmas of progress that when we take steps forward there are steps which are sacrificed in its name. What is born of progress is ultimately replaced by it. We should be mindful, however, that progress does not necessarily translate into societal improvement, nor guarantee it. Such was the case of America's passenger train.

While we try to recapture and focus the memories we seek a paradise lost, but in so doing we come to realize that the wonder of the memories is in the details. So seek out the cars, the terminals and the museums. They are transportation's treasures for those who remember them and intriguing industrial relics for those who do not. Nevertheless, the terminals and the cars are *master pieces* of design *to be* treasured. The Great Steel Fleet *was great* and though we may regret its passing, we can be thankful that it will always remain as an important part of our heritage.

Geoffrey H. Dough

On the author's annual journey aboard the *New England States* in 1967, he caught the baggage handler observing the train's 6:23 AM departure from a very foggy Utica, New York. The train glided quietly and smoothly into the mist.

Glossary

ALCO	American Locomotive Company - Builders of steam and diesel locomotives.
Big Four	The Cleveland, Cincinnati, Chicago and St. Louis Railroad. A NYC subsidiary.
Budd	Edward G. Budd Manufacturing, or "Budd" Company, builders of patented shot weld design stainless steel lightweight passengers cars.
Buffet/Lounge	A car which contains a lounge section, and a sequestered section with tables where light snacks and beverages are served; sometimes referenced as a tavern/lounge. At times the lounge section became a "parlor."
Compartment	A room slightly larger than a bedroom which contained a sofa, chairs and enclosed lavatory.
Consist	The cars that make up a train.
Drawing room	A large bedroom for two or three persons.
EMD	Electro-Motive Division of General Motors, builders of diesel locomotives (originally EMC - Electro Motive Corporation).
E7	Designation for EMD passenger units (locomotives) purchased by NYC 1945-1949, rated at 2000 hp, Nos. 4000-4035(A units); 4100-4113 (B units).
E8	Designation for EMD passenger units purchased by NYC 1950-1953, rated at 2250hp, Nos. 4036-4095.
GP	EMD "General Purpose" followed by numerical designation, 7 or 9, to indicate horsepower rating, 1500hp and 1750hp respectively; often equipped with steam generator to run in passenger service (to provide heat, AC an d electric).
Grill-diner	A self-contained dining car which served less expensive cuisine, sandwiches, beverages and lighter fare, containing 44 seats. Half the dining section had a section of tables facing inward while the other half contained standard tables and chairs.
NYC	New York Central
Nickel Plate	The New York, Chicago and St. Louis Railroad (NYC & StL).
10-5	10-roomette/5-double bedroom car built by Pullman 1937-1939.
10-6	10-roomette/6-double bedroom car built by Pullman-Standard and Budd.
4-4-2	A sleeping car built by Pullman 1937-1939 contain 4-bedrooms, 4-compartments and 2-drawing rooms.
Observation	The rear car of a train which allowed passengers to sit in a lounge with a 180 degree ability to view the traveled path of the train.
PA	ALCO P (passenger) A (A-locomotive with cab controls) B (cabless booster engine). PA-1:2000hp passenger unit; PA-2: 2250hp passenger unit. NYC purchased four PA-1s in 1948, Nos. 4200-4203; PB-1s 4300-4302; and six PA-2s in 1950-51, Nos. 4208-4212 and PB-2 4304.
Parlor	A car with separate plush seating, facing inward or outward arrayed in two rows on each side of the car. A special surcharge was assessed for a parlor car seat.
Pennsy	The Pennsylvania Railroad.
Pullman Company	Operating Division of Pullman, Inc. which serviced, staffed and leased the cars built by Pullman-Standard to the railroads in North America.
Pullman-Standard	Manufacturing division of Pullman which built passenger and freight equipment.
Schedule	That part of a timetable which prescribes the class, direction, number and movement for a regular train.
Section	A Pullman accommodation in a sleeping car which contained two sofas facing each other, or one sofa against the side of the car facing inward, which converted to sleeping berths, a lower and/or an upper.
Sleeper	A passenger car containing sleeping accommodations sometimes referred to as a "Pullman," as in "Pullman Cars only."
Standard	Cars built before the streamline era of the "standard" design, containing sections, compartments, bedrooms and/or drawing rooms, riding on six wheel trucks. The primary distinction is their weight, hence they are known as "heavyweight" cars.
Tail sign	The sign on the rear of the observation car or end of train which displays the name of the train. Sometimes called a "drumhead."
Tavern-Lounge	See Buffet/lounge
Unit	A diesel locomotive, with or without cab controls.

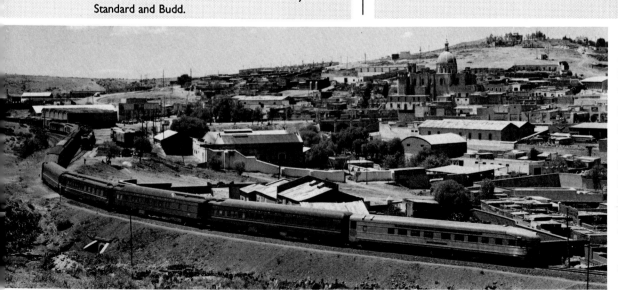

NdeM operated its ex-NYC parlor-lounge-observations across its system. One is seen here on August 18, 1962 at Zacatecas, Mexico. The observation has been named "Club Central."

Victor Hand

Victor Hand

NdeM's *El Regiomontano* is christened by officials and dedicated in November 1962. The car is ex-NYC *Manhattan Island*, built for the 1938 *20th Century Limited*.

On July 22, 1968, Penn Central operated its Empire Service between New York City and Buffalo. Four such trains meet at Albany, including the Delaware and Hudson's *Laurentian*, led by PA-1 No. 19. Albany Union Station survives in 1995, but the tracks and platforms are gone.

Victor Hand

No.	To	Date	Disposition
9100			Retired 1953, believed wrecked
9101			Retired 1976, to Amtrak Work Train No. 17013
9102	Amtrak 1180	1974	
9103			Retired between 1971 and 1976. All except 4 (sold to AFT) scrapped
9104			Retired 1974, Sold to American Freedom Train (AFT) for display car, renumbered 110
9105	Amtrak 1126	1976	
9106	Amtrak 1127	1976	
9107	Amtrak 1128	1976	
9108	Amtrak 1181	1974	
9109			Retired between 1971 and 1976.
9110	Amtrak 1120	1976	
9111	Amtrak 1121	1976	
9112	Amtrak 1182	1974	
9113	Amtrak 1183	1974	
9114	Amtrak 1125	1976	
9115			Retired 1974, Sold to American Freedom Train (AFT) for display car, renumbered 104
9116	Amtrak 1184	1974	
9117			Retired 1976, to Amtrak Work Train No. 17014
9118	Amtrak 1122	1976	
9119			
9120	Amtrak 1185	1974	
9121	Amtrak 1186	1974	
9122			Retired between 1971 and 1976.
9123	Amtrak 1187	1974	
9124	Amtrak 1188	1974	Retired 1976, wrecked, scrapped
9125			Retired 1976, to Amtrak Work Train No. 17015
9126			Retired 1976, to Amtrak Work Train No. 17016
9127	Amtrak 1189	1974	
9128			Retired 1974, Sold to American Freedom Train (AFT) for display car, renumbered 101
9129	Amtrak 1129	1976	
9130			Retired 1976, to Amtrak Work Train No. 17017
9131	Amtrak 1191	1974	
9132	Amtrak 1192	1974	
9133			Retired 1974, Sold to American Freedom Train (AFT) for crew car, renumbered 99, later 20
9135			Retired 1974, Sold to American Freedom Train (AFT) for display car, renumbered 105
9134	Amtrak 1130	1976	
9136	Amtrak 1131	1976	
9137			Retired between 1971 and 1976.
9138			Retired 1974, Sold to American Freedom Train (AFT) for display car, renumbered 107
9139			Retired 1974, Sold to American Freedom Train (AFT) for display car, renumbered 108
9140	Amtrak 1123	1976	
9141	Amtrak 1132	1976	
9142			Retired 1976, to Amtrak Work Train No. 17018
9143			Retired 1976, to Amtrak Work Train No. 17019
9144			Retired 1976, to Amtrak Work Train No. 17020
9145			Retired between 1971 and 1976.
9146	Amtrak 1133	1976	
9147			Retired 1976, to Amtrak Work Train No. 17021
9148			Retired 1959, believed wrecked
9149	Amtrak 1193	1974	
9150			Retired 1964, believed wrecked
9151	Amtrak 1124	1976	Converted to Head End Power Car No. 693 in 1977
9152			Retired between 1971 and 1976.
9153			Retired 1976, to Amtrak Work Train No. 17022
9154			Retired between 1971 and 1976.
9155	Amtrak 1134	1976	
9156			Retired 1974, Sold to American Freedom Train (AFT) for display car, renumbered 106
9157			Retired 1976, to Amtrak Work Train No. 17023
9158			Retired 1974, Sold to American Freedom Train (AFT) for display car, renumbered 102
9159			Retired 1976, to Amtrak Work Train No. 17024
9160			Retired between 1971 and 1976.
9161	Amtrak 1135	1976	
9162	Amtrak 1136	1976	
9163			Retired 1974, Sold to American Freedom Train (AFT) for control car, renumbered 100
9164	Amtrak 1137	1976	
9165			Retired 1974, Sold to American Freedom Train (AFT) for display car, renumbered 109
9166	Amtrak 1138	1976	
9167			Retired between 1971 and 1976.
9168			Retired between 1971 and 1976.
9169	Amtrak 1194	1974	
9170	Amtrak 1139	1976	
9171	Amtrak 1195	1974	
9172	Amtrak 1140	1976	
9173	Amtrak 1141	1976	
9174			Retired 1966, believed wrecked
9175	Amtrak 1196	1974	
9176			Retired between 1971 and 1976.
9177			Retired 1976, to Amtrak Work Train No. 17025
9178			Retired 1974, Sold to American Freedom Train (AFT) for display car, renumbered 103
9179			Retired 1976, to Amtrak Work Train No. 17026
9180	Amtrak 1142	1976	

ACF 100 Cars Baggage Plan/Lot 2910 Ordered 9/45, 12/45 Delivered 10/46, 5/47, continued

No.	To	Date	Disposition
9181	Amtrak 1197	1974	
9182			Retired 1976, to Amtrak Work Train No. 17027
9183			Retired 1976, to Amtrak Work Train No. 17028
9184			Retired 1976, to Amtrak Work Train No. 17029
9185			Retired 1968, believed wrecked
9186			Retired between 1971 and 1976.
9187	Amtrak 1143	1976	
9188	Amtrak 1144	1976	
9189	Amtrak 1145	1976	
9190			Retired between 1971 and 1976.
9191	Amtrak 1198	1974	
9192	Amtrak 1146	1976	
9193			Retired between 1971 and 1976.
9194			Retired between 1971 and 1976.
9195	Amtrak 1199	1974	
9196			Retired between 1971 and 1976.
9197			Retired between 1971 and 1976.
9198			Retired 1976, to Amtrak Work Train No. 17030

ACF 2 Cars Baggage/30' Mail Plan/Lot 2958 Ordered 12/45 Delivered 7/47

No.	To	Date	Disposition
5014			Retired 1967, scrapped
5015			Retired 1967, sold to Ted Church, Erie Pennsylvania

ACF 4 Cars Baggage/60' Mail Plan/Lot 2959 Ordered 12/45 Delivered 7/47

No.	To	Date	Disposition
4907			Retired 1966, scrapped
4908			Retired 1967, scrapped
4909			Retired 1967, scrapped
4910			Retired 1962, scrapped

ACF 2 Cars Baggage/48 Seat Coach Plan/Lot 2960 Ordered 12/45 Delivered 4/47

No.	To	Date	Disposition
344			Retired 1966, Sold to Ted Church, Erie Pennsylvania
345			Retired 1964, scrapped

ACF 20 Cars Baggage/48 Seat Coach Plan/Lot 2730 Ordered 5/44 Delivered 2/47, 3/47

No.	To	Date	Disposition
280			Retired 1964-1968, scrapped
281			Retired 1964-1968, scrapped
282			Retired 1964-1968, scrapped
283			Retired 1964-1968, scrapped
284			Retired 1964-1968, scrapped
285			Retired 1964-1968, scrapped
286			Retired 1964-1968, scrapped
287			Retired 1964-1968, scrapped
288			Retired 1964-1968, scrapped
289			Retired 1964-1968, scrapped
290			Retired 1964-1968, Sold to Ted Church, Erie, Pennsylvania
291			Retired 1964-1968, scrapped
292			Retired 1964-1968, scrapped
293			Retired 1964-1968, scrapped
294			Retired 1964-1968, scrapped
295			Retired 1964-1968, scrapped
296			Retired 1964-1968, scrapped
297			Retired 1964-1968, scrapped
298			Retired 1964-1968, scrapped
299			Retired 1964-1968, scrapped

Budd Empire State Express Cars Ordered 1/41 Delivered 11/41

No./Name	Type	Plan/Lot	re '52	PC	Disposition
Alonzo B. Cornell	Bagg/60' Mail	96209	5021	6500	Retired 1971, sold to Strates Bros. Circus
John W. Dix	"		5022	6501	Retired 1971, sold to Strates Bros. Circus
Grover Cleveland	Bagg/Bar	96208	33	--	Retired 1961, sold to NdeM
Martin Van Buren	"		34	--	Retired 1961, sold to NdeM

Built as 56 seat coach. Converted to 108 seat coach in 1966. Numbers applied in 1952, renumbered in 1966.

Number/Name		Type	Plan/Lot	re '66	PC	Disposition
2570	Reuben E. Fenton	Coach	96204	1710	2110	Unknown
2571	Hamilton Fish	"	"	1705	2105	Rochester Chapter NRHS
2572	David B. Hill	"	"	1707	2107	Rochester Chapter NRHS
2573	Morgan Lewis	"	"	1702	2102	Unknown
2574	William I. Marcy	"	"	1713	2113	Unknown
2575	Edwin D. Morgan	"	"	1704	2104	Unknown
2576	William R. Seward	"	"	1708	2108	Unknown

Budd Empire State Express Cars Ordered 1/41 Delivered 11/41, continued

Number/Name		Type	Plan/Lot	re '66	PC	Disposition
2577	Daniel D. Tompkins	"	"	1709	2109	Unknown
2578	Charles S. Whitman	"	"	1701	2101	Rochester Chapter NRHS
2579	Silas Wright	"	"	1714	2114	Unknown
2565		"	"	1712	2112	Unknown
2566		"	"	1703	2103	Rochester Chapter NRHS
2567		"	"	1711	2111	Unknown
2568		"	"	1700	2100	Rochester Chapter NRHS
2569		"	"	1706	2106	Unknown
2564	Thomas E. Dewey (Named in 1954)	"				Retired 1965, sold to Livonia Avon and Lakeview Railroad

Empire State Express   Ordered 1/41, Delivered 11/41

No./Name	Type	Plan/Lot	1952	PC	Disposition
Theodore Roosevelt	Obs/Bar/Lounge	96205	54		Retired 1958, sold to NdeM
Franklin D. Roosevelt	"	"	55		Retired 1958 , sold to NdeM
George Clinton	44 seat Diner	96206	686		Retired 1960, sold to NdeM
DeWitt Clinton	"	"	687		Retired 1960, sold to NdeM
John Jay	"	"	688		Retired 1960, sold to NdeM
Horatio Seymour	"	"	689		Retired 1959, sold to NdeM

30 Seat parlor/5 Seat Drawing Room

	Type	Plan/Lot	1952	PC	Disposition
Samuel J. Tilden	Parlor/Dr. Rm	96207	86		To Long Island No. 530, 1967. Converted to Commuter Bar/24 Seat Lounge. Retired 1974, scrapped.
Alfred E. Smith	"	"	85		Retired 1961, Sold to Jones Properties
Nathan Miller	"	"	83		Retired 1961, Sold to Jones Properties
Charles E. Hughes	"	"	81		Retired 1961, Sold to Jones Properties
Herbert H. Lehman	"	"	82	7123	To Amtrak 3600, 1971; converted to coach 1972, re 3600, re 5698, retired 1976 Converted to 56 seat coach No. 5698, 1973. Retired 1976, scrapped
Levi P. Morton	"	"	84	7124	To Amtrak 3601, 1971; converted to coach 1973, re 3601, re 5699, sold to Western New York Historical Society

Budd Pool Cars   Ordered 3/44, Delivered 11/47-12/47

Built as Buffet 47 seat lounge cars. In 1966 car nos. 38 and 39 had five lounge seats removed and replaced with coat and luggage racks for use as parlor cars.

No./Name	Type	Plan/Lot	PC	Amtrak 1976	Disposition
35	Buffet-Lounge	9608-004	--	--	Wrecked 1964
36	"	"	--	--	Converted to Meal-A-Mat in 1963, wrecked in 1966
37	"	"	4437	--	To NJ DOT 4437 in 1976
38	"	"	4438	3346	Retired 1977, to work train No. 10310
39	"	"	4439	--	To NJ DOT 4439 in 1976
40	"	"	4440	--	To NJ DOT 4440 in 1976
41	"	"	--	--	Wrecked 1967
42	"	"	--		Converted to Meal-A-Mat in 1963, retired 1967, scrapped
43	"	"	4443	--	To NJ DOT 4443 in 1976
44	"	"	4444	3347	Retired 1977, to work train No. 10311
45	"	"	--	--	Retired 1964, sold to James E. Strates Shows
46	"	"	4446	--	To NJ DOT 4446 in 1976
47	"	"	4447		

Budd Pool Cars   Ordered 3/44, Delivered 11/47-12/47

Built as 56 seat coaches. Except where noted, all cars transferred to Penn Central retaining assigned numbers.

No./Name	Type	Plan/Lot	Amtrak	Year	Disposition
900	56 seat Coach	9613-004	5640	1974	Denver Railcar Co.
901	"	"	5641	"	Denver Railcar Co.
902	"	"	5642	"	Retired 1977, Sold to Maine Central for work train service
904	"	"	5643	"	Unknown
905	"	"	5675	1973	Unknown
906	"	"	5644	1974	Unknown
908	"	"	5645	"	Retired 1977, scrapped
909	"	"	5646	"	Denver Railcar Co.
910	"	"	5647	"	Retired 1976, scrapped
911	"	"	5648	"	Unknown
913	"	"	5649	"	Unknown
914	"	"	5650	"	Unknown
915	"	"	5651	"	Unknown
916	"	"	5676	1973	Unknown
918	"	"	5677	"	Unknown
919	"	"	5652	1974	Unknown
922	"	"	5653	"	Unknown
924	"	"	5654	"	Retired 1977, scrapped
925	"	"	5678	1973	Unknown
926	"	"	5655	1974	Unknown
927	"	"	5679	1973	Unknown
928	"	"	5656	1974	Unknown
930	"	"	5657	1974	Unknown

Built as 56 seat coaches. Except where noted, all cars transferred to Penn Central retaining assigned numbers.

No./Name	Type	Plan/Lot	Amtrak	Year	Disposition
2931	"	"	5680	1973	Unknown
2932	"	"	5681	"	Unknown
2933	"	"	5658	1974	Mohawk & Hudson Chapter NRHS
2934	"	"	5659	"	Unknown
2937	"	"	5660	"	Denver Railcar Co.
2939	"	"	5661	"	Retired 1979, destroyed by fire
2941	"	"	5682	1973	Unknown
2942	"	"	5662	1974	Unknown
2943	"	"	5683	1973	Unknown
2944	"	"	5663	1974	Sold to Denver Railcar Co.
2945	"	"	5684	1973	Unknown
2946	"	"	5664	1974	Unknown
2947	"	"	5665	"	Sold to Denver Railcar Co.
2948	"	"	5666	"	Unknown
2949	"	"	5667	"	Unknown
2950	"	"	5668	"	Unknown
2951	"	"	5669	"	Unknown
2953	"	"	5685	1973	Unknown
2954	"	"	5670	1974	Unknown
2955	"	"	5671	"	Unknown
2957	"	"	5672	"	Unknown
2958	"	"	5673	"	Unknown
2959	"	"	5674	"	Unknown

No./Name	Type	Plan/Lot	PRR/PC	Amtrak	Disposition
2903	56 Seat Coach	9613-004	1425	5630	To Amtrak 1974
2912	"	"	1426	5633	To Amtrak 1974
2917	"	"	1427	5631	To Amtrak 1974, retired 1977, scrapped
2920	"	"	1428	5632	To Amtrak 1974
2921	"	"	1429	5634	To Amtrak 1976, retired 1977; soldl to Dixie Railroad Corp.
2923	"	"	1430	5635	To Amtrak 1976, retired 1977, held
2907	"	"			Retired 1971, wrecked
2936	"	"			Retired 1971, sold to High Iron Co.; sold to Morristown & Erie Railway
2940	"	"			Retired 1971, wrecked
2938	"	"			Sold to Long Island RR in 1967, converted to 106 seat coach No. 529, retired 1972, scrapped
2952	"	"			Retired 1966, sold to Livonia Avon & Lakeville RR
2929, 2935, 2956	"	"			One car wrecked 1960, remainder retired 1966, scrapped

Budd Pool Cars Ordered 12/45, Delivered 9/47-10/47, except as noted

Built as Baggage/Dormitory. One car wrecked 1961, remainder retired 1964-68 and converted to work train service.

No./Name	Type	Plan/Lot	Disposition
8970	Baggage/Dormitory	9614-023	
8971	"	"	
8972	"	"	
8973	"	"	
8974	"	"	
8975	"	"	
8976	"	"	
8977	"	"	
8978	"	"	Retired 1968, worktrain X27279
8979	"	"	
8980	"	9614-004	Ordered 3/44
8981	"	"	Ordered 3/44

Budd Pool Cars Delivered 11/47-12/47, except as noted - Built as 44 seat diners

No./Name	Type	Plan/Lot	Ordered	PC	Disposition
447	44 Seat Diner	9624-023	12/45		Retired 1967, Work Train Service
448	"	"	"	4548	Retired 1969, Sold to High Iron Co.
449	"	"	"	4549	Retired 1969 Sold to Choo Choo Hilton, Chattanooga, Tennessee
694	44 Seat Diner	9624-004	Ord 3/44	4545	To Amtrak 8029, 1973 Retired 1976, scrapped
696	"	"	"	4546	Retired 1969 Sold to Choo Choo Hilton, Chattanooga, Tennessee
698	"	"	"	4547	Retired 1969 Sold to Choo Choo Hilton, Chattanooga, Tennessee
691	"	"	"		Retired 1965, scrapped
692	"	"	"		Retired 1965, scrapped
693	"	"	"		Retired 1965, scrapped
695	"	"	"		Retired 1965, scrapped
697	"	"	"		Retired 1965, Sold to Jones Properties
699	"	"	"		Retired 1965, Sold to Jones Properties

Budd Pool Cars Ordered 3/44, Delivered 3/48-5/48

Built as 44-Seat Diner/Grill. Cars sold to Amtrak converted to 24 seat diner/20 seat lounge; rebuilt to 44 seat diners.

No./Name	Type	Plan/Lot	PC	Amtrak	Disposition
450	44 Seat Diner/Grill		4550	8330	Amtrak 1973, re 8519, in service, 6/95
452	"		4552	8331	Amtrak 1973, re 8553, in service, 6/95
453	"		4553	8332	Amtrak 1973, retired
454	"		4554	8333	Amtrak 1973, re 8333, in service, 6/95
455	"		4555		Retired 1971, sold to NdeM
456	"		4556		Retired 1971, sold to Choo Choo Hilton: Volunteer
457	"		4557	8339	Amtrak 1973, re 8515, in service, 6/95
460	"		4560		Retired 1971, scrapped
461	"		4561	8336	Amtrak renumbered in 1973, retired
463	"		4563	8335	Amtrak 1973, re 8512, in service, 6/95
464	"		4564	8334	Amtrak 1973, re 8556, in service, 6/95
465	"		4565	8337	Amtrak 1973, re 8513, in service, 6/95
466	"		4566	8338	Amtrak 1973, re 8514, in service, 6/95

451, 458, 459, 462, 467   1 retired 1960, 2 retired 1966, 2 retired 1968. All scrapped

Budd Pool Cars Ordered 3/44, Delivered 8/47-10/47

Built as Kitchen/22 seat lounge. Cars coupled with companion 64 seat dining car. Jones Properties, owner of Pickens Railroad leased all cars to Canadian National before CN assumed ownership.

No./Name	Type	Plan/Lot	Companion Diner	Disposition
478	Kitchen/Lounge	9643-023	405	Pickens 605 in 1967, CN in 1969, retired 1977, scrapped
479	"	"	404	Retired 1967, scrapped
480	"	"	406	Retired 1968, sold to High Iron Company; Texas Southern Ry.; sold to Washington Central
481	"	"	408	Pickens 607 in 1964, CN in 1964, retired 1968, scrapped
482	"	"	407	Pickens 601 in 1967, CN in 1969, retired 1977, scrapped
483	"	"	487	Pickens 611 in 1965, CN in 1969, retired 1977, scrapped
484	"	9643-004	490	Pickens 609 in 1966, CN in 1969, retired 1977, scrapped
485	"	"	489	Pickens 603 in 1964, CN in 1969, retired 1977, scrapped
486	"	"	488	PC 4591, to SCL 5981 in 1970, retired 1971, scrapped

Budd Ordered 3/44, Delivered 2/48

Built as Observation/Buffet 53 seat lounge. All cars sold to Kansas City Southern in 1960, renumbered in 1963 when converted to 32 seat lounge, 8 seat lunch counter. All cars retired 1970.

No./Name	Type	Plan/Lot	KCS	Re '63	Disposition
48	Obs/Buffet/Lounge	9634-004	44	43	Sold to Wm. Dodd, Baton Rouge, Louisiana; sold to J. F. Williams, renamed "Starlight Forty-eight"
49	"	"	45	44	Sold to Wm. Dodd, Baton Rouge, Louisiana
50	"	"	46	40	Sold to Wm.B. Stuart of Riley Boosters Club; Kasten Railcar Services
51	"	"	47	42	Sold to Brewton Lumber, Winfield, Louisiana

Budd Ordered 3/44, Delivered 4/48-6/48

Built as Observation/10 seat lounge, 30 seat parlor. All cars sold to NdeM except as noted.

No./Name	Type	Plan/Lot	Amtrak	Disposition
58	Obs/Lounge/Parlor	9638-004		Retired 1959
59	"	"		Retired 1958
60	"	"	3860	Renumbered 1972, scrapped
61	"	"		Retired 1965, sold to Johnnies Vets Club, Des Moines, Iowa; Texas Dinner Train; sold to Denver Railcar Co.
62	"	"		Retired 1958
63	"	"		Retired 1958
64	"	"		Retired 1958
65	"	"		Retired 1958
66	"	"		Retired 1964
67	"	"	3871	Renumbered 1972, scrapped
68	"	"		Retired 1958
69	"	"		Retired 1958
70	"	"		Retired 1961

Budd Sleepers Ordered 12/45, Delivered 1/49-3/49 - 10 Roomettes/ 6 Bedroom Sleeper

No	Name	Plan/Lot	PC	Amtrak	Disposition
10100	Mohawk Valley	9510/9660-023			Retired 1968, sold to NdeM
10101	Morning Valley	"			Retired 1967, wrecked
10102	Navajo Valley	"	4252	2834	Amtrak 1973, retired
10103	Orchard Valley	"			Retired 1968, sold to NdeM
10104	Onondaga Valley	"			Retired 1968, wrecked
10105	San Joaquin Valley	"			Retired 1968, sold to NdeM
10106	Peaceful Valley	"			Retired 1968, scrapped
10107	Peach Valley	"			Retired 1968, scrapped
10108	Round Valley	"			Retired 1966, sold to NdeM
10109	Scitoharie Valley	"			Retired 1968, sold to NdeM
10110	Sonoma Valley	"			Retired 1966, sold to NdeM
10111	Eden Valley	9502/9662-023			Retired 1966, sold to Gueringer Tours
10112	Eventide Valley	"			Retired 1968, scrapped
10113	Keuka Valley	"			Retired 1968, sold to NdeM

Budd Sleepers Ordered 12/45, Delivered 1/49-3/49 - 10 Roomettes/ 6 Bedroom Sleeper, continued

No	Name	Plan/Lot	PC	Amtrak	Disposition
10114	Pine Valley	9510/9660-023	4259	2835	Amtrak 1973, retired 1976, scrapped
10115	Tully Valley	"			Retired 1968, scrapped
10116	Yosemite Valley	"	4261		Retired 1971, scrapped
10117	Zoar Valley	"	4262		Retired 1971, scrapped
10118	Canary Valley	9502/9662-023			Retired 1967, sold to NdeM
10119	Cedar Valley	"			Retired 1968, sold to NdeM
10120	Champlain Valley	"			Retired 1968, sold to NdeM
10121	Caribou Valley	"	4265		Retired 1971, scrapped
10122	Klamath Valley	"	4266	2830	Amtrak 1973, retired 1976, scrapped
10123	Lebanon Valley	"	4267	2831	Amtrak 1973, retired sold to Great Steel Fleet Rail
10124	Maumee Valley	"			Retired 1968, scrapped
10125	Meadow Valley	"			Retired 1968, sold to NdeM
10126	Castle Valley	"			Retired 1968, sold to Indiana Railroad Museum
10127	Central Valley	"			Retired 1967, scrapped
10128	Genesee Valley	"			Retired 1968, scrapped
10129	Keene Valley	"	4271	2832	Amtrak 1973, retired
10130	Cumberland Valley	"			Retired 1968, sold to NdeM
10131	Hunting Valley	"			Retired 1967, sold to NdeM
10132	Cherry Valley	"	4273		Retired 1971, scrapped
10133	Happy Valley	"			Retired 1968, sold to NdeM
10134	Chagrin Valley	"			Retired 1968, sold to NdeM
10135	Minnesota Valley	9510/9660-023			Retired 1967, scrapped
10136	Missouri Valley	"	4276	2836	Amtrak re 1973, retired
10137	Maple Valley	9502/9662-023	4277	2833	Amtrak re 1973, retired, scrapped
10138	Skyland Valley	9510/9660-023			Retired 1966, sold to NdeM
10139	Putnam Valley	"			Retired 1968, scrapped

Budd Sleepers Ordered 12/45, Delivered 1/49-3/49 - 22 Roomettes

No.	Name	Plan/Lot	Re '61	PC	Disposition
10350	Albany Harbor	9501/9661-023			Retired 1966, sold to NdeM
10351	Ashtabula Harbor	"			Retired 1966, sold to NdeM : Presa Chique
10352	Bar Harbor	"			Retired 1968, sold to NdeM
10353	Benton Harbor	"			Retired 1968, sold to NdeM
10354	Boothbay Harbor	"			Retired 1968, sold to NdeM
10355	Boston Harbor	"			Retired 1967, sold to NdeM : Presa Tenango
10356	Buffalo Harbor	"			Retired 1966, sold to NdeM
10357	Cape Vincent Harbor	"			Retired 1966, sold to NdeM : Presa Infiernillo
10358	Charlotte Harbor	"			Retired 1967, sold to NdeM
10359	Cheboygan Harbor	"			Retired 1966, sold to NdeM
10360*	Fairport Harbor	"	10812	4202	Amtrak 2001 in 1971, re 2051, active 6/95
10361	Gary Harbor	"			Retired 1966, sold to NdeM
10362	Cleveland Harbor	"			Retired 1966, sold to NdeM
10363	Conneaut Harbor	"			Retired 1966, sold to NdeM
10364*	Dunkirk Harbor	"	10810	4200	Amtrak 2000 in 1971, re 2052, stored 5/4/95
10365*	Erie Harbor	"	10811		Retired 1968, scrapped
10366	Michigan Harbor	"			Retired 1966, sold to NdeM
10367*	Monroe Harbor	"	10814	4204	Amtrak 2002 in 1971, re 2050, active 6/95
10368	Henderson Harbor	"			Retired 1967, sold to NdeM
10369	Home Harbor	"			Retired 1967, sold to NdeM
10370*	Indiana Harbor	"	10813		Retired 1968, scrapped
10371	Mackinac Harbor	"			Retired 1966, sold to NdeM
10372*	Vermillion Harbor	"	10818	4208	Amtrak 2006 in 1971, re 2056, wrecked at Batavia NY, 1995
10373*	York Harbor	"	10819		Retired 1968, scrapped
10374	Oak Harbor	"			Retired 1966, sold to NdeM
10375	Ogdensburg Harbor	"			Retired 1967, sold to NdeM
10376	Sacketts harbor	"			Retired 1966, sold to NdeM
10377*	South Haven Harbor	"	10815	4205	Amtrak 2003 in 1971, re 2054, stored
10378	Tarrytown Harbor	"			Retired 1966, sold to NdeM
10379*	Toledo Harbor	"	10816	4206	Amtrak 2004 in 1971, re 2056, stored 8/30/94, Beech Grove
10380*	Tonawanda Harbor	"	10817	4207	Amtrak 2005 in 1971, re 2053, sold

* Rebuilt to sleepercoaches in 8/61 - 10/61

Budd Sleeper/Observation Lounge Ordered 12/45, Delivered 6/49-7/49 - 5 Bedrooms, Observation-Lounge Cars

No.	Name	Plan/Lot	Re '58	Amtrak	Disposition
10564	Singing Brook	9508/9636-023	10630		Sold to Canadian Pacific in 1959, renamed Mountain View; sold to Algoma Central, renamed "Canyon View"Sold to Milwaukee Railcar, Texas & Buffalo and Steamship Co. "Danny Taggert"
10565	Sunrise Brook	"	10631		Retired 1964, sold to Jones Properties
10566	Wingate Brook	"	10632	3260	Amtrak re 1972, retired sold to Kasten Railcar Service

Budd Sleeper/Buffet/Lounge Ordered 12/45, Delivered 3/49-5/49 - 6 Bedrooms/Buffet/22 Seat Lounge

No.	Name	Plan/Lot	Renumbered	PC	Disposition
10620	Forest Stream	9505/9663-023		4411	Re Amtrak 3200 in 1971
10621	Gulf Stream	"	657	4416	Re '66, Re Amtrak 3205 in 1973, sold to WDME Radio in Dover-Foxcroft, Maine
10622	Rapid Stream	"	663	4417	Re Amtrak 3206 in 1973
10623	Rippling Stream	"	658	4418	Re '66, Re Amtrak 3209 in 1974

Budd Sleeper/Buffet/Lounge Ordered 12/45, Delivered 3/49-5/49 - 6 Bedrooms/Buffet/22 Seat Lounge, continued

No.	Name	Plan/Lot	Renumbered	PC	Disposition
0624	Boulder Stream	"	656	4419	Re '66, Re Amtrak 3208 in 1974, sold to Dixie Railcar Corp., Savannah, Georgia
0625	Crystal Stream	"	661	4414	Re '67, Re Amtrak 3203 in 1973
0626	Woodland Stream	"		4412	Re Amtrak 3202 in 1971, Sold to Richard Kostura
0627	Swift Stream	"	660	4415	Re '67, Re Amtrak 3204 in 1973, Sold to Michael K. Fox "City of Angels"
0628	Laurel Stream	"		4413	Re Amtrak 3201 in 1971, sold to New Orleans Chapter, NRHS
0629	Mountain Stream	"	659	4423	Re '67, Re Amtrak 3207 in 1974
0630	Rainbow Stream	"			Retired 1966, scrapped

Budd Sleeper/Observation/Buffet/Lounge Ordered 12/45, Delivered 5/49-6/49

5 Bedrooms, Observation, Buffet, 25 seat lounge. All cars are operating today in the US.

No.	Name	Plan/Lot	Disposition
0560	Babbling Brook	9506/9664-023	Sold to Canadian Pacific in 1959, renamed Seaview Retired 1969, sold to Quebec Cartier Mining, re 847; Mid-America Railcar Service
0561	Bonnie Brook	"	Retired 1964, sold to Fred Corriher, Landis, South Carolina, New Orleans Chapter NRHS
0562	Fall Brook	"	Sold to Canadian Pacific in 1959, renamed Eastview; Retired 1969, sold to United Railroad Supply, Montreal, QuebecSold to Casablanca Fan Corp.; Sold to Anschutz Corp., renamed "Colorado"
0563	Plum Brook	"	Sold to Canadian Pacific in 1959, renamed Seaview Retired 1969, sold to Quebec Cartier Mining, renumbered 846; sold to Carolina Rail Ltd.; Sold to Pennsylvania Pullmans, Inc.

Budd Sleepercoach Ordered 10/59, Delivered 10/'59

24 single room, 8 double room. All cars leased to NYC, sold to Northern Pacific

No.	Type	Plan/Lot	NP	Amtrak	Disposition
0800	Sleepercoach	9540/9691-040	333	2031	NP named Loch Tay in 1964, Amtrak re 1971, re 2089, sold
0801	"	"	334	2032	NP name Loch Rannoch 1964, Amtrak re 1971, re 2082, active 6/95
0802	"	"	335	2033	NP named Loch Arkaig in 1964, Amtrak re 1971, re 2092, active 6/95
0803	"	"	336	2034	NP named Loch Awe in 1964, Amtrak re 1971, re 2083, sold

Pullman-Standard Baggage/Dormitory Ordered 12/45, Delivered 3/48-5/48

No.	Type	Plan/Lot	Disposition
961	Baggage/Dormitory	7543/6789	Sold to CRI&P in 1959, re 821, retired 1968 Sold to Ringling Brothers Circus
962	"	"	Sold to CRI&P in 1959, re 822, retired 1968 Sold to Ringling Brothers Circus
963	"	"	Retired 1959, scrapped
964	"	"	Retired 1968, scrapped
965	"	"	Retired 1964, to work train service No. 24211
966	"	"	Retired 1964, to work train service No. 24212
967	"	"	Sold to CRI&P in 1959, re 823, retired 1968 Sold to Ringling Brothers Circus
968	"	"	Retired 1964, scrapped
969	"	"	Retired 1961, scrapped

Pullman-Standard Ordered 12/45, Delivered 7/48-8/48 - 68 seat diners

No.	Type	Plan/Lot	Amtrak	Disposition
00	68 Seat Diner	7544/6789	4584	Converted 1954 to 64 seat diner, 6 seat waiting lounge Coupled to 476, assigned to Commodore Vanderbilt Retired 1971, scrapped
01	"	"		Converted 1950 to 64 seat diner, 6 seat waiting lounge Coupled to 474, assigned to 20th Century Limited Retired 1960, scrapped
02	"	"	4585	Converted 1954 to 64 seat diner, 6 seat waiting lounge Coupled to 477, assigned to Commodore Vanderbilt Retired 1971, scrapped
03	"	"		Converted 1950 to 64 seat diner, 6 seat waiting lounge Coupled to 475, assigned to 20th Century Limited Retired 1960, scrapped
76	Kitchen/23 seat Lounge	7545/6789	4586	Coupled to 400 (above) Retired 1971, scrapped
77	"	"	4587	Coupled to 402 (above) Retired 1971, scrapped
74	Kitchen/Dormitory	7546/6789		Coupled to 401 (above) Retired 1960, scrapped
75	"	"		Coupled to 403 (above) Retired 1960, used in Detroit wreck train service now CR 45905

Pullman-Standard Ordered 12/45, Delivered 7/48-8/48 - 44 seat diners

No.	Type	Plan/Lot	PC	Disposition
440	44 Seat Diner	7547/6789		Retired 1966, scrapped
441	"	"		Wrecked 1961, sold to Delaware & Hudson,
				Sold to Cooperstown & Charlotte Valley Ry., 1972
442	"	"		Retired 1966, scrapped
443	"	"		Retired 1966, scrapped
444	"	"		Retired 1968, scrapped
445	"	"		Retired 1966, scrapped
446	"	"		Retired 1966, scrapped

Pullman-Standard Ordered 12/45, Delivered 7/48-8/48

Buffet/30 seat lounge/Secretary/Barber/Telephone/Shower

No.	Type	Plan/Lot	Rock Island	Disposition
10572	Atlantic Shore	7548/6789	481	Sold to Rock Island 1959, named Pacific Shore, retired 1975
				Sold to Kennedy Farms;
				Sold 1984 to Western New York Historical Society
10573	Lake Shore	"	482	Sold to Rock Island 1959, retaining same name
				Retired 1971, scrapped

Note: Rock Island changed interior configuration to 4 seat room to replace Barber room, 2 seat room to replace Train secretary room, buffet, 24 seat lounge. Cars redecorated in 1961 with a 28 seat lounge. Shower and telephone not used.

Pullman-Standard Ordered 12/45, Delivered 7/48-8/48 - 6 Bedroom/Buffet/22 Seat Lounge

No.	Type	Plan/Lot	Re	Year	Disposition
10600	Big Moose Lake	4124/6790	653	1965	Retired 1967, sold to Tyler Robbins, Cleveland, Ohio
10601	Cayuga Lake	"			Retired 1961, scrapped
10602	Cranberry Lake	"			Retired 1966, sold to Jones Properties
10603	Mirror Lake	"	652	1964	Retired 1967, sold to Ted Church, Erie, Pennsylvania
10604	Oneida Lake	"			Retired 1961, sold to Jones Properties
10605	Otisco Lake	"			Retired 1964, scrapped
10606	Otsego Lake	"	651	1964	Retired 1967, used in Toledo wreck train
10607	Otter Lake	"			Retired 1961, scrapped
10608	Raquette Lake	"	654	1965	Retired 1968, scrapped
10609	Saranac Lake	"	1598	1966	PC 4422, Converted to 3 Day Rooms, Commuter Bar
					Each room contained 4 seat card table plus usual bedroom sofa
10610	Seneca Lake	"			Retired 1961, scrapped
10611	Silver Lake	"			Retired 1961, scrapped
10612	Skaneateles Lake	"			Retired 1961, scrapped
10613	Trout Lake	"			Retired 1961, scrapped
10614	Tupper Lake	"	655	1966	Retired 1967
					Sold to General Electric as a Test Car
10615	Walton Lake	"	1597	1966	PC 4421 Converted to 3 Day Rooms, Commuter Bar
					Each room contained 4 seat card table plus usual bedroom sofa

Pullman-Standard Ordered 12/45, Delivered 10/48 - 22 Roomette

No.	Name	Plan/Lot	IC	Year	Disposition
10400	Caminada Bay	4122/6790			To Canadian National 2052 1958, renamed Val Alain. Converted to 52 seat "Dayniter" and renumbered 5733 in 1977
10401	Cape Cod Bay	"			To CRI&P No. 866 in 1959, converted to baggage, retired 1968
					Sold to Ringling Brothers Circus
10402	Tampa Bay	"			Wrecked 1958.
10403	Tawas Bay	"	1820	1962	Converted to Baggage, retired 1971, scrapped
10404	Traverse Bay	"			To Canadian National 2055 1958, renamed Val Cote. Converted to 52 seat "Dayniter" and renumbered 5734 in 1977
10405	Three Mile Bay	"			To Canadian National 2061 1958, renamed Valhalla. Converted to baggage/dormitory (14 roomettes) renumbered 9485 in 1973
10406	James Bay	"			To Canadian National 2064 1958, renamed Val Marie. Converted to 52 seat "Dayniter" and renumbered 5737 in 1977
10407	Little Neck Bay	"	1999	1959	To Illinois Central 1959, converted to Dormitory.
					Converted 1960 to Baggage/60' mail, mail section removed 1968, renumbered 1830, retired 1971, scrapped
10408	Manhasset Bay	"	151	1961	Converted to Baggage/60' mail, mail section removed 1968, renumbered 1831, retired 1971, scrapped
10409	Nahant Bay	"			To CRI&P No. 755 in 1959, converted to baggage/60' mail, retired 1968, sold to Ringling Brothers Circus
10410	New York Bay	"			To CRI&P No. 756 in 1959, converted to baggage/60' mail, retired 1968, sold to Ringling Brothers Circus
10411	Pigeon Bay	"			To Canadian National 2073 1958, renamed Val Rose. Converted to baggage/dormitory (14 roomettes) renumbered 9488 in 1974
10412	Quincy Bay	"			To Canadian National 2072 1958, renamed Val Royal.
					Wrecked 1965.
10413	Raritan Bay	"			To CRI&P No. 757 in 1959, converted to baggage/60' mail, retired 1968, sold to Ringling Brothers Circus
10414	Saginaw Bay	"			To CRI&P No. 758 in 1959, converted to baggage/60' mail, retired 1968, sold to Ringling Brothers Circus
10415	Turtle Bay	"	157	1964	To Illinois Central, 1959 "Fernwood"
					Converted 1964 to Baggage/60' mail, mail section removed 1968, renumbered 1837, retired 1971, scrapped

Pullman-Standard Ordered 12/45, Delivered 10/48 - 22 Roomette

No.	Name	Plan/Lot	IC	Year	Disposition
10416	Peekskill Bay	"			To CRI&P No. 867 in 1959, converted to baggage, retired 1968 Sold to Ringling Brothers Circus
10417	Haverstraw Bay	"			To Canadian National 2069 1958, renamed Valrita. Converted to baggage/dormitory (14 roomettes) renumbered 9486 in 1974, Global Communications; sold 1986 to Bluewater Chapter NRHS
10418	Humber Bay	"			To Canadian National 2066 1958, renamed Valois. Converted to baggage/dormitory (14 roomettes) renumbered 9478 in 1973
10419	Smithtown Bay	"			To Canadian National 2074 1958, renamed Val St. Michael. Converted to baggage/dormitory (14 roomettes) renumbered 9481 in 1973; to VIA in 1978; scrapped 7/1995
10420	Sodus Bay	"			To Canadian National 2058 1958, renamed Vacourt. Converted to 52 seat "Dayniter" and renumbered 5738 in 1977; to VIA in 1978, stored 1995.
10421	Birch Bay	"			To CRI&P No. 864 in 1959, converted to baggage, retired 1968 Sold to Ringling Brothers Circus
10422	Delaware Bay	"			To Canadian National 2068 1958, renamed Valpoy. Converted to baggage/dormitory (14 roomettes) renumbered 9480 in 1973
10423	Dorcas Bay	"			To Canadian National 2053 1958, renamed Val Brilliant. Converted to baggage/dormitory (14 roomettes) renumbered 9482 in 1973
10424	Dorchester Bay	"			To Canadian National 2060 1958, renamed Val Doucet. Converted to baggage/dormitory (14 roomettes) renumbered 9484 in 1973
10425	Chesapeake Bay	"			To Canadian National 2062 1958, renamed Val Jalbert. Converted to 52 seat "Dayniter" and renumbered 5736 in 1977
10426	Chippewa Bay	"	4202	1964	To Illinois Central, 1959 Renamed Flossmoor Converted 1964 to 10 seat lounge chair/16 seat diner/16 seat lounge
10427	Sandusky Bay	"	4203	1966	To Illinois Central, 1959 Renamed Fort Dodge, Converted 1964 to 10 seat lounge chair/16 seat diner/16 seat lounge Wrecked at Tonti, Illinois 1971
10428	Sandy Hook Bay	"			To Canadian Nation 2054 1958, renamed Val Cartier. Converted to baggage/dormitory (14 roomettes) renumbered 9476 in 1973
10429	Mexico Bay	"			To CRI&P No. 759 in 1959, converted to baggage/60' mail, retired 1968, sold to Ringling Brothers Circus
10430	Gardiners Bay	"			To Canadian National 2056 1958, renamed Val Alain. Converted to 52 seat "Dayniter" and renumbered 5735 in 1977
10431	Mobile Bay	"	156	1963	To Illinois Central, 1959 renamed Fulton. Converted 1963 to Baggage/60' mail, mail section removed 1970, renumbered to 1840, retired 1971, scrapped
10432	Monterrey Bay	"	155	1963	Converted to Baggage/60' mail, mail section removed 1968, renumbered 1835, wrecked 1968, Lodi, Illinois
10433	San Francisco Bay	"			To Canadian National 2070 1958, renamed Val St. Patrick. Converted to baggage/dormitory (14 roomettes) renumbered 9475 in 1973
10434	Sheepshead Bay	"			To Canadian National 2071 1958, renamed Val Gagne. Converted to baggage/dormitory (14 roomettes) renumbered 9487 in 1973
10435	Huntington Bay	"			To Canadian National 2057 1958, renamed Val d 'Amour. Converted to baggage/dormitory (14 roomettes) and renumbered 9483 in 1973; retired - sold
10436	Jamaica Bay	"			To CRI&P No. 865 in 1959, converted to baggage, retired 1968 Sold to Ringling Brothers Circus
10437	Casco Bay	"			To Canadian National 2059 1958, renamed Val d'Espoir. Converted to 52 seat "Dayniter" and renumbered 5732 in 1977
10438	Chaumont Bay	"			To Canadian National 2065 1958, renamed Valmont. Wrecked 1962 and destroyed by fire.
10439	Wild Fowl Bay	"	1821	1962	Converted to Baggage, retired 1971, scrapped
10440	Willoughby Bay	"			To CRI&P No. 754 in 1959, converted to baggage/60' mail, retired 1968, sold to Ringling Brothers Circus
10441	Great South Bay	"	152	1961	Converted to Baggage/60' mail, mail section removed 1968, renumbered 1832, retired 1971, scrapped
10442	Great Peconic Bay	"			To Canadian National 2063 1958, renamed Valjean. Converted to baggage/dormitory (14 roomettes) renumbered 9477 in 1973
10443	Thunder Bay	"			To Canadian National 2067 1958, renamed Valpariso. Converted to baggage/dormitory (14 roomettes) renumbered 9479 in 1973
10444	Sturgeon Bay	"	1822	1962	Converted to Baggage, wrecked 1971, Tonti, Illinois

Pullman-Standard Ordered 12/45, Delivered 4/49 - 5/49 - 12 Bedroom Sleeper

No.	Type	Plan/Lot	PC	Disposition
10500	Port of Buffalo	4125/6790		Retired 1968, sold to Ringling Brothers Circus
10501	Port Byron	"		Retired 1968, sold to Ringling Borthers Circus
10502	Port of Albany	"		Retired 1968, sold to Judge Hofheinz
10503	Port of Boston	"		Retired 1968, sold to Judge Hofheinz
10504	Port of Lewiston	"		Wrecked 1968
10505	Port Orange	"		Retired 1968, sold to Jones Properties
10506	Port of Oswego	"		Retired 1966, sold to Jones Properties
10507	Port of Windsor	"		Retired 1968, sold to Lake Shore Chapter NRHS
10508	Port of New York	"		Retired 1968, sold to Ringling Brothers Circus
10509	Port Lawrence	"		Wrecked 1968
10510	Port Clinton	"		Retired 1968, sold to Ted Church, Erie, Pennsylvania; sold to Western New York Historical Society
10511	Port of Detroit	"		Retired 1968, sold to Judge Hofheinz
10512	Port of Chicago	"		Retired 1968, scrapped
10513	Port Chester	"		Retired 1966, sold to Jones Properties

Note: All cars except 10504 and 10505 initially equipped with electric braking for Twentieth Century Limited service.

10 Roomette/6 Bedroom Sleeper. All cars sold to CN, NdeM or FCP as indicated.

No.	Name	Plan/Lot	CN	Disposition
10140	Calumet River*	4123/6790		Retired 1963, to NdeM Siria
10141	Powder River*	"	2075	To CN 1965, renamed Exploits River
10142	Platte River*	"		Retired 1966, to NdeM Iran
10143	Portage River	"		Retired 1966, scrapped
10144	Penobscot River*	"	2076	To CN 1965, renamed Margaree River
10145	Perch River*	"		Retired 1965, to NdeM Arabia
10146	Muskingum River	"		Retired 1963, to FCP Aries
10147	Mystic River	"		Wrecked 1960
10148	Neponset River	"		Retired 1968, scrapped
10149	Gila River	"		Retired 1964, to NdeM Espania
10150	Grass River	"		Retired 1964, to NdeM Suiza
10151	Farmington River	"		Retired 1964, to NdeM Alemenia
10152	Miami River	"	2077	To CN 1965, renamed Mabou River
10153	Beaver River	"		Retired 1964, to NdeM Islandia
10154	Blanchard River	"		Retired 1963, to FCP Ursa Major
10155	Des Moines River	"		Retired 1964, to NdeM Rumania
10156	Des Plains River	"		Retired 1964, to NdeM Italia
10157	Winding River	"	2078	To CN 1965, renamed Sable River
10158	Illinois River	"		Retired 1966, to NdeM Turquia
10159	Little Fox River	"		Retired 1964, to NdeM Finlandia
10160	Little Miami River	"		Retired 1964, to NdeM Checoeslovaquia
10161	Agawam River	"	2079	To CN 1965, renamed Restigouche River
10162	Deer River	"	2080	To CN 1965, renamed Petitcodiac River
10163	Little Osage River	"		Retired 1964, to NdeM Yugoslovia
10164	Detroit River	"		Retired 1963, to FCP Polaris
10165	East River	"	2081	To CN 1965, renamed Rivere de Loup
10166	Mahoning River	"		Retired 1964, to NdeM Grecia
10167	Manistee River	"	2082	To CN 1965, renamed Rivere de au Renard; to VIA 1978; to Met-Recy Ltee 8/1983; sol to Salem & Hillsborough RR, sold to a restaurant in Dalhousie, N.B. scrapped 1994.
10168	Elkhart River	"		Retired 1964, to FCP Capricornus
10169	Indian River	"		Retired 1966, to NdeM Sumatra
10170	Bronx River	"		Retired 1965, to NdeM Morruecos
10171	Current River	"		Retired 1968, scrapped
10172	Bonnie Femme River	"		Retired 1963, to FCP Cassiopedia
10173	Burbois River	"		Retired 1965, to NdeM Afghanistan
10174	St. Regis River	"	2083	To CN 1965, renamed Rivere Rouge; Sold to John H. Deasy, converted to 6-bedroom lounge.
10175	Swan River	"		Retired 1966, to NdeM Chipre
10176	Rouge River	"		Retired 1966, to FCP Libra
10177	Sabine River	"		Retired 1964, to FCP Gemini
10178	Feather River	"		Retired 1965, to NdeM Egipto
10179	North River	"		Retired 1966, to NdeM Yemen
10188	St. Francis River	"	2084	To CN 1965, renamed Rivere Raquette; sold to Memphis Transportation Museum
10180	Neshannock River	"		Retired 1964, to FCP Aquarius
10181	Niantic River	"		Retired 1966, to NdeM Libano
10182	Thames River	"		Retired 1966, to NdeM Israel
10183	Raisin River	"		Retired 1964, to NdeM Portugal
10184	Shenango River	"		Retired 1963, to NdeM Thalandia
10185	Sparkling River	"		Retired 1965, to NdeM Argelia
10186	St. Clair River	"		Retired 1964, to NdeM Inglaterra
10187	St. Croix River	"		Retired 1965, to NdeM Pakistan
10189	St. Joseph River	"		Retired 1965, to NdeM Birmania
10190	Croton River	"		Retired 1964, scrapped
10191	Aroostock River	"		Retired 1965, to NdeM Irak
10192	Ausable River	"		Retired 1967, scrapped
10193	Harlem River	"		Retired 1964, to NdeM Paises Bazos
10194	Monongahela River	"		Retired 1965, to NdeM Nepal
10195	Roanoke River	"		Retired 1965, to NdeM Cachemira
10196	Rocky River	"		Retired 1964, to NdeM Polomia
10197	Licking River	"	2085	To CN 1965, renamed Nipigon River; off roster 11/86
10198	Merrimack River	"		Retired 1964, to NdeM Austria
10199	Chicopee River	"	2086	To CN 1965, renamed Pembina River
10200	Clinton River*	"		Retired 1965, to NdeM Corea
10201	Pecos River*	"		Retired 1966, to NdeM Sudan
10202	Chateaugau River*	"		Retired 1964, to NdeM Rusia
10203	Chicago River*	"		Retired 1963, to NdeM Taurus
10204	Sacandaga River	"		Retired 1965, to NdeM Jordania
10205	Salmon River	"		Retired 1963, to FCP Sirius
10206	Iroquois River	"		Retired 1964, to NdeM Albania
10207	Kalamazoo River	"		Retired 1965, to NdeM Camboya
10208	Allegheny River	"		Retired 1964, to NdeM Dinamarco
10209	Amazon River	"		Retired 1964, to NdeM Bulgaria
10210	Westfield River	"		Retired 1968, scrapped
10211	Whitewater River	"		Retired 1964, to NdeM Norvega
10212	Willamette River	"		Retired 1965, to NdeM Ceylan
10213	Hocking River	"	2087	To CN 1965, renamed Saskatchewan River; Sold to Hartwell-Lowe Co., converted to 8-6 "Norma Peterson"
10214	Hudson River	"		Retired 1964, to NdeM Francia
10215	Huron River	"	2088	To CN 1965, renamed Prairie River
10216	Housatonic River	"	2089	To CN 1965, renamed Peace River

Pullman-Standard Ordered 12/45, Delivered 9/48 - 3/49, continued

10 Roomette/6 Bedroom Sleeper. All cars sold to CN, NdeM or FCP as indicated.

No.	Name	Plan/Lot	CN	Disposition
10217	Connecticut River*	"		Retired 1966, to NdeM Oman
10218	Niagara River	"	2090	To CN 1965, renamed Smoky River; Sold to Kasten Railcar
10219	Thornapple River	"		Retired 1964, to FCP Leo
10220	Cass River*	"		Wrecked 1960
10221	Sangamon River	"		Retired 1966, to NdeM Etiopia
10222	Saugus River	"	2091	To CN 1965, renamed Skeena River
				To inspection car Sandford Fleming in 1975
10223	Scioto River	"	2092	To CN 1965, renamed Hay River
10224	St. Lawrence River	"		Retired 1964, to NdeM Hungria
10225	St. Marys River	"		Retired 1964, to NdeM Tibet
10226	Stillwater River	"		Retired 1964, to FCP Saggitarious
10227	Tiffin River	"		Retired 1965, to NdeM Tunez
10228	Tippecanoe River	"		Retired 1963, to FCP Ursa Minor
10229	Trinity River	"		Retired 1965, to NdeM Laos
10230	Oswegatchie River	"	2093	To CN 1965, renamed Yukon River
10231	Oswego River	"		Retired 1964, to FCP Piscis
10232	Ottawa river	"		Retired 1964, to NdeM Suecia
10233	Kankakee River	"	2094	To CN 1965, renamed Rideau River
10234	Kings River	"		Retired 1964, to NdeM Belgica
10235	Passaic River*	"		Retired 1965, to NdeM India
10236	Roundout River	"		Retired 1964, to NdeM Islanda

* Indicates car was originally equipped with electric braking for Twentieth Century Limited service.

Pullman-Standard Ordered 12/45, Delivered 8/48 - 9/48

5 Bedroom/Observation Buffet/23 seat lounge

No.	Name	Plan/Lot	Re 1958	Disposition
10570	Hickory Creek	4126/6790	10633	Retired 1968, sold to Ringling Brothers Circus; Sold to Black River & Western
105471	Sandy Creek	"	10634	Retired 1968, sold to Indiana Railroad Museum; Sold to American Orient Express 1990

Pullman-Standard Ordered 11/46 by Chesapeake and Ohio, Delivered 8/50

No.	Name	Plan/Lot	Disposition
470	Kitchen/Dormitory	7607/6859	Coupled with 411, to Illinois Central 4127A in 1956
			Retired 1969, sold to Gilchrist Tractor Co.
471	"	"	Coupled with 412, to Illinois Central 4128A in 1956
			Retired 1968, sold to David Wallace; 1990 Texas Dinner Train, Texas Southern Railway
472	"	"	Coupled with 409, to B&O 1093 in 1957.
			Retired 1969, to Shay Inn Restaurant, Cass West Virginia
473	"	"	Coupled with 410, to B&O 1095 in 1957
			Retired 1969, scrapped
411	52 Seat Diner	7605/6860	To IC 4127 in 1956; Retired 1969; Sold to Gilchrist Tractor Co.
412	"	"	To IC 4128 in 1956, Retired 1969, sold to David Wallace; 1990 Texas Dinner Train
409	"	"	To B&O 1092 in 1957, Retired 1969, to Shay Inn Restaurant, Cass West Virginia
410	"	"	To B&O 1094 in 1957, Converted to Instruction Car

Note: IC converted the dining car to a 68 seat diner. B&O converted the dining car to a 64 seat diner as originally constructed.

Kansas City Southern bought NYC observation lounge No. 51. Shown here on Train 10 at New Orleans, Louisiana on May 28, 1967 as KCS 42.

J. W. Swanberg

COACHES FORWARD
37 38
TO REAR
35 36 34 33

Wallace W. Abbey, Courtesy Trains Magazin

Cincinnati Union Terminal, September 25, 1952